Allen Ginsberg

Revised Edition

By Thomas F. Merrill

University of Delaware

Twayne Publishers
A Division of G. K. Hall & Co. • *Boston*

1-0231

Allen Ginsberg, Revised Edition

Thomas F. Merrill

Copyright 1988 by G.K. Hall & Co.
All rights reserved.
Published by Twayne Publishers
A Division of G.K. Hall & Co.
70 Lincoln Street
Boston, Massachusetts 02111

Copyediting supervised by Lewis DeSimone
Book production by Gabrielle B. McDonald
Book design by Barbara Anderson

Typeset in 11 pt. Garamond
by P&M Typesetting, Inc., Waterbury, Connecticut

Printed on permanent/durable acid-free paper
and bound in the United States of America

Library of Congress Cataloging in Publication Data

Merrill, Thomas F.
  Allen Ginsberg.

  (Twayne's United States authors series ; TUSAS 161)
  Bibliography: p.
  Includes index.
  1. Ginsberg, Allen, 1926–   —Criticism and
interpretation. I. Title. II. Series.
PS3513.I74Z74 1988   811'.54   87-23686
ISBN 0-8057-7510-2 (alk. paper)

Contents

About the Author

Thomas F. Merrill was born in Maplewood, New Jersey, in 1932. He was educated at Blair Academy, Princeton University (A.B.), the University of Nebraska (M.A.), and the University of Wisconsin (Ph.D.). He was a captain in the Strategic Air Command, serving on a B-47 combat crew. Merrill has taught at the University of Wisconsin, U.C.L.A., DePauw University and, as a Visiting Fulbright Lecturer, at the Université de Bordeaux and the Collège Litteraire de Pau. Currently professor of English at the University of Delaware, he is the author of *Epic God-talk: Paradise Lost and the Grammar of Religious Language* (1986), *The Poetry of Charles Olson: A Primer* (1982), *Christian Criticism: A Study of Literary God-talk* (1976), and *William Perkins: 1558–1602* (1966). He is married and has four children.

Preface

On 13 October 1955, amid literary friends and jugs of cheap wine at the Six Gallery in San Francisco, Allen Ginsberg began a legend with the first public reading of *Howl*. It was, says John Tytell, "like a detonation in a museum."[1] The Beat Generation had found its voice, and the museum has never been the same. Notoriety and litigation followed. *Howl* became a cause célèbre in the fifties and its author a countercultural institution and magnet for the media, ever thirsty for eye-catching exemplars of cultural change. For an unsuspecting popular audience, the poem recorded the despair and desolation of a strange and threatening population of "angelheaded hipsters," who were alienated, disaffiliated, and "destroyed by madness, starving hysterical naked, / dragging themselves through the negro streets at dawn looking for an angry fix."

More than a quarter of a century later, *Howl* seems, as one reviewer puts it, "no more threatening than a cap pistol."[2] Indeed, times have changed, and even Ginsberg in the eighties when he again reads—this time to audiences who marvel that "he looks like any college professor"—reads a *Howl* that is no longer a threatening manifesto, but a comic satire. "In Europe, where 100,000 Prague youths once elected Ginsberg King Of May," muses one eyewitness, "the young are once again marching against war. On campuses there are teach-ins about the threat of nuclear holocaust. But this night, at this Columbia campus, . . . Allen Ginsberg is chatting, singing, wearing a necktie and making his howl a thigh-slapping hoot. . . . He plays a worn squeeze-box and sings: 'Meditate on emptiness, 'cause that's where you're going, and how.' "[3]

This poet, whose work is one long "life-poem" of public and private experience, has traveled a harrowing journey from angry protest to serene Buddhist "emptiness." It is the aim of this book to chart that journey through the poems, pointing out with as much critical objectivity as possible, the literary points of interest along the way.

The first chapter concerns the philosophical, psychological, and social atmosphere of what in the fifties was called the Beat Generation. Chapter Two, drawing an aesthetic from the premises of the first, attempts to show that the literary theory of beat writers springs directly from their philosophical attitudes. Succeeding chapters address the major published volumes of Ginsberg's poetry up to the present. Chapter Nine recapitulates some of the principles of postmodernist literary theory in order to form a context for understanding Ginsberg's achievement.

Since virtually all the notable published work has been collected in *Collected Poems: 1947–1980,* all citations to poems quoted or discussed refer to this volume and will appear parenthetically in the text.

Thomas F. Merrill

University of Delaware

Acknowledgments

I wish to thank once again City Lights Books, Corinth Books, Inc., Viking Press, Inc., the *Paris Review,* and Harper & Row for permission to quote from poetry and interviews, and the University of Delaware General Research Fund for support during the revision of this study.

Chronology

1926   Allen Ginsberg born 3 June, Newark, New Jersey. His mother, Naomi, was a Russian émigré; and his father, Louis Ginsberg, a lyric poet and teacher in the school district of Paterson, New Jersey.

1943   Ginsberg leaves Paterson High School at the age of seventeen to attend Columbia University.

1945   Ginsberg is dismissed from Columbia. Completes four-month program at Merchant Marine Academy, Sheepshead Bay, Brooklyn.

1946   Ships out on seven-month voyage stopping at ports on the Atlantic and Gulf coasts.

1947   Visits Neal Cassady in Denver, Colorado; ships out on the freighter *John Blair* to Africa via Marseilles, causing him to miss registration for fall classes at Columbia.

1948   Readmitted to Columbia and graduates with a bachelor of arts degree and an A − scholastic average; remains at Columbia for graduate study.

1948–1949   Experiences a series of mystic visions of William Blake, the first beginning in a sublet tenement apartment in Harlem.

1949   Becomes inadvertently involved in criminal activities of Herbert Huncke and, in lieu of jail, undergoes psychiatric counseling followed by an eight-month stay at Rockland (New York) State Hospital for psychoanalysis and therapy where he meets Carl Solomon.

1950   Returns to Paterson to live with his father. Works as a book reviewer for *Newsweek* and a market research consultant. Interviews and befriends William Carlos Williams.

1953–1955   Hitchhikes to Key West and flies first to Cuba and then to Yucatan to explore Mayan ruins. Stays at the plantation of Karena Shields where he writes "Siesta at

Xbalba." Relocates to San Francisco, where he suffers final break with Neal Cassady. Begins friendship with Peter Orlovsky.

1956–1959   Publication of *Howl and Other Poems* by City Lights Books. Subsequent litigation leads to "obscenity trial" and eventual verdict that the book is not obscene. Ginsberg takes trips to the Arctic, Tangier, Venice, Amsterdam, Paris, London, and Oxford. Begins series of poetry readings at various universities including Harvard, Columbia, and Princeton. Completes *Kaddish* and records *Howl* for Fantasy records.

[handwritten margin note: mother dies]

1960   Experiments with *yage* drug in Peruvian jungles and writes of his experiences to William Burroughs. Has terrifying visions of a Death/God.

1961   Publishes *Empty Mirror* and begins trip to Far East. Meets with Martin Buber and various oriental holy men. Appears as actor in motion picture *Pull My Daisy*. *Kaddish and Other Poems* published by City Lights Books.

1962   Appears in second motion picture, *Guns of the Trees*.

1963   Undergoes change in his basic attitude toward existence, which is recorded in the poem "The Change: Kyoto-Tokyo Express." *Reality Sandwiches* published by City Lights Books; also (with William Burroughs) *The Yage Letters*.

1965   European tour. Crowned *Kral Majales* (King of May) by Czech students in Prague before expulsion for political activism.

1965–1966   Guggenheim Fellowship; National Endowment for the Arts grant.

1966   *Wichita Vortex Sutra*. *Paris Review* interview.

1967   Appears in movie *Chappaqua*.

1968   *Planet News* (City Lights Books); *T.V. Baby Poems; Ankor Wat*.

1969   *Airplane Dreams: Compositions from Journals*.

1969   National Institute of Arts and Letters award.

1970   *Notes after an Evening with William Carlos Williams; Indian Journals: March 1962–May 1963.*

1971   *Ginsberg's Improvised Poetics.*

1972   Begins long association with Chögyam Trungpa, a spiritual teacher of Buddhist meditational practices. Arrested for engaging in "passive resistance demonstrations" at the Republican National Convention in Miami. City Lights Books publishes *The Fall of America: Poems of These States 1965–1971;* and Grey Fox Press, *The Gates of Wrath: Rhymed Poems, 1948–1952.*

1974   Cofounds the Jack Kerouac School of Disembodied Poetics as part of the Naropa Institute, a Buddhist university established by Chögyam Trungpa at Boulder, Colorado. Wins National Book Award for *The Fall of America.* Publication of *Iron Horse; Allen Verbatim: Lectures on Poetry, Politics, Consciousness; The Visions of the Great Rememberer.*

1975   *Chicago Trial Testimony* and *First Blues, Rags, Ballads & Harmonium Songs 1971–74.* Performs a number of spontaneously composed blues songs as "poet-percussionist" with Bob Dylan in a cross-country musical tour called the "Rolling Thunder Review."

1977   *Journals, Early Fifties-Early Sixties.*

1978   Arrested during antinuclear demonstration at Rocky Flats, Colorado. *Poems All Over the Place: Mostly Seventies; Mind Breaths: Poems 1972–1977.*

1979   National Arts Club Gold Medal.

1982   *Plutonian Ode.*

1984   *Collected Poems: 1947–1980.*

1986   *White Shroud: Poems 1980–1985; Howl: Original Draft Facsimile,* edited by Barry Miles.

Chapter One
Ginsberg and the Beat Attitude

Allen Ginsberg's collection of early poems *The Empty Mirror* begins with a poetic statement of the profoundest fatigue and hopelessness; but the mood is religious:

> I feel as if I am at a dead
> end and so I am finished.
> All spiritual facts I realize
> are true but I never escape
> the feeling of being closed in
> and the sordidness of self,
> the futility of all that I
> have seen and done and said.
> Maybe if I continued things
> would please me more but now
> I have no hope and I am tired.
>
> (*CP*, 71)

The poem expresses not exultation, not the certitude of a life that has found comfort in the evidence of things unseen, but the mood of a spirit that has long been besieged by doubts and has experienced a face-to-face encounter with the enervating specter of despair. "I am tired," the poet says, and in this weariness we hear the echo of the existentialist complaints so familiar to us in the modern age. Kierkegaard might have diagnosed the malady as the "sickness unto death"; Jack Kerouac gave it a hipster christening: "beat."

Like existentialism, the definitive boundaries of "beat" have been blurred both by the variety of attitudes that they enclose and by the notoriety that the popular press has brought to the term. The world is all too familiar with the "beatnik," but it is less so with the philosophy behind the beard and sandals. To be beat in the fifties was to feel the bored fatigue of the soldier required to perform endless, meaningless tasks that have no purpose. Society imposed authority from without, but beatniks obeyed an authority from within. Viewed as a social phenomenon, they appeared "fed up" and recalcitrant— grumbling malcontents and irresponsible hedonists. Inwardly the case was quite different. There the beatniks regarded themselves as pioneers, explorers of interior reality; in this respect, they resembled traditional religious mystics. Paul Portugés, in fact, explores what he calls Ginsberg's "visionary poetics" in the context of Christian mysticism, although he cautions that "one distinctive feature of Ginsberg's visions (and Blake's to some extent) is that they are directed toward the poetry and the poetics and *not* toward an ultimate, divine saviour."[1] The beats' much sensationalized use of drugs and hallucinogens only illustrates that their quest for inward reality had taken advantage of the resources of modern science. They could easily see themselves as jet-age Saint Johns of the Cross.[2]

The incessant search for reality within (through drugs, meditation, and intense feeling) was a quest for authenticity that reason, it was felt, deadened. It called for reconnaissance at the extremes of human experience, as far beyond the limits of reason as possible, thus placing uncommon stress upon subjective moods. Truth, for the beats as for Kierkegaard, was "an appropriation process of the most passionate inwardness." Unlike the rationalist they would not attempt to overcome their fears, guilt, dread, and cares; rather, they exploited these feelings in order to reach new levels of truth about themselves. Moods, they passionately believed, were indices to reality.

Obviously, such a commitment to internal truth not only permits but demands the uninhibited confessions that tend to make conventional readers squirm. Many beat writers, especially Ginsberg, flaunt their most intimate acts and feelings—masturbation, sodomy, drug addiction, erotic dreams—in aggressively explicit street language. To the social conservative, it is shameless exhibitionism. To the beats, such expression is the denial of shame itself, a manifesto that nothing human or personal can be degrading. If this attitude seems uncivil, even childish, consider Blake's assurance that "the fool who persists in his folly will become wise."[3]

John P. Sisk says that the beats were "locked in a dialectic" with society;[4] that is, they assumed the role of a nonbelligerent opposition, meeting the rigid rationalism of society with deliberate irrationality. It was nonbelligerent because the Beat Generation had no interest in resistance, in crusade, in movements, or in any activity, for that matter, that remotely resembled fighting. The beats were indifferent enemies of society but enemies nonetheless; because they were appalled by the ugliness of its materialism and goals and the emptiness of its values. They were indifferent because they had come to believe that they could not change society—change could only come from within. So beatniks chose not to fight. In the battle for social, spiritual, and aesthetic progress, they were conscientious objectors. They played it "cool"; they sought to "make the scene" as best they could.

Disaffiliation and Death

The words that were most often used to describe this posture were *disaffiliation* and *disengagement*. These are uneasy words to a nation of joiners where the number of organizations one belongs to can determine success as much as intellectual or occupational achievement. As Paul O'Neil rather bluntly puts it, the beats felt that "the only way man can call his soul his own is by becoming an outcast."[5] True, they were outcasts from society but intensely bound by friendships. The loose bonding of the social contract was superseded by the "responsible resoluteness of an inter-personal fidelity."[6]

Because they felt modern society had mangled the concepts of *self* and *neighbor* into grotesque hypocrisies that reduce "civilized" living to an immense lie, the beats disaffiliated for the purpose of making "interpersonal fidelity" possible. Ginsberg documents his own awakening to this "lie." In the Columbia university bookstore one day, it suddenly came to him that everyone there was concealing an unconscious torment from one another: "they all looked like horrible grotesque masks, grotesque because *hiding* the knowledge from each other."[7]

The vision of people "*hiding* the knowledge from one another" testifies to the beat conviction that people are more real (and presumably better) than society allows them to be and also that collective society has an awesome control over people that transcends their individual wills. The truth about humanity—the truth that society obdurately censors—is shouted by Ginsberg in his "Footnote to *Howl*": "Everything is holy! everybody's holy! everywhere is holy! everyday is in eternity! Everyman's an angel!" (*CP,* 134).

Religion

The beat writers generally shared a freestyle religiosity. Jack Kerouac, for instance, was concerned to emphasize his beat religious calling: "No, I want to speak *for* things, for the crucifix I speak out, for the Star of Israel I speak out, for the divinest man who ever lived who was a German (Bach) I speak out, for sweet Mohammed I speak out, for Buddha I speak out, for Lao-tse and Chuang-tse I speak out,"[8] but Gary Snyder maps its religious contours best: "[I find] three things going on: 1. *Vision and illumination-seeking*. This is most easily done by systematic experimentation with narcotics. . . . 2. *Love, respect for life, abandon, Whitman, pacifism, anarchism, etc.* . . . partly responsible for the mystique of 'angels,' the glorification of skid-row and hitchhiking, and a kind of mindless enthusiasm. . . . 3. *Discipline, aesthetics, and tradition* . . . its practitioners settle on one traditional religion, try to absorb the feel of its art and history, and carry out whatever ascesis is required."[9] The Church was "square," but religious sensitivity was "hip." On the occasions when the beat writers did use Judeo-Christian concepts, they exploited them with a fanatical application that knew no compromise. "Everyman is Holy, Every day is in eternity! Everyman's an angel!" (*CP*, 134) bellowed Ginsberg over the blare of a saxophone. The offense of all this to organized religion was basically its lack of discipline, decorum, and its general disregard for traditional ethical teachings. Theologically, there was not so much disparity as one would expect.

Beats were prone to religious illumination. Kerouac reports, "I went one afternoon to the church of my childhood . . . and suddenly with tears in my eyes had a vision of what I must have really meant with 'Beat' . . . the vision of the word Beat as being to mean beatific."[10] But Allen Ginsberg's famous vision in a subleased apartment in Spanish Harlem of William Blake is an even more sensational example. So arresting was this experience for the poet that his spiritual-aesthetic existence orbited around it for the next fifteen years of his life.[11] "I wasn't even reading, my eye was idling over the page of *The Sunflower*," Ginsberg explains, "and it suddenly appeared . . . and suddenly I realized that the poem was talking about *me*. . . . Now, I began understanding it, . . . and suddenly, simultaneously with understanding it, heard a very deep earthen grave voice in the room, which I immediately assumed, I didn't think twice, was Blake's voice. . . . But the peculiar quality of the voice was something unforgettable because it was like God had a human voice, with all the infinite tenderness and anciency and mortal gravity of a living Creator speaking to his son."[12]

The essential religious matrix of the beats, however, was in the

Orient. Because of its conception of the holiness of personal impulse (which often was interpreted as sanction for doing whatever came naturally), Zen Buddhism was particularly attractive. Every impulse of the soul, the psyche, and the heart was one of holiness. Everything was holy if understood as such, a point Ginsberg hammered home through repetition in his "Footnote to *Howl*":

> Holy! Holy! Holy! Holy! Holy! Holy! Holy! Holy!
> Holy! Holy! Holy! Holy! Holy! Holy! Holy!
> The world is holy! The soul is holy! The skin
> is holy! The nose is holy! . . .
>
> *(CP, 134)*

Whatever the source—Judaism, Whitman, Buddhism, Saint John of the Cross—here is radical sacred egalitarianism, a statement that nothing is profane and that therefore no human act is not of God. As blanket a denial of evil as is possible, it represents a genuine fusion of Western and Eastern theological attitudes. The Judeo-Christian dualism of good versus evil is obliterated by a oriental relativism that neatly does away with the consequences of the spiritual pride that has bloodied the pages of Western ecclesiastical history.

The alternative to ethical dualism is a sense of the natural balance of things: an appreciation not of good versus evil but of good and evil. In the *Hsin-hsin Ming* or "Treatise on Faith in the Mind," a poem attributed to Seng-ts'an, a sixth-century Zen master, can be found the following words:

> If you want to get the plain truth
> Be not concerned with right and wrong
> The conflict between right and wrong
> Is the sickness of the mind.[13]

The view represented by this fragment, that the conflict between right and wrong is an unnecessary and harmful concern, had enormous appeal for beat writers. The basic corruption of the "square world," as they saw it, was its compulsion to be right. This compulsion had done great harm in Western cultural history, because it had insisted upon a perspective of ethical dualism in which good had always been set in taut opposition to bad with the result that people had suffered the burdens of shame and guilt, which seemed to them the most significant by-products of Western cultural psychology. And, shame and guilt were considered overwhelming obstacles to a view of life that celebrated the holy integrity of humanity and the world.

Buddhism

According to Zen, evil is not considered the natural enemy of good but its inevitable companion. They are sides of the same coin, and the proper stance of a reasonable person toward them is not to pursue one and resist the other but to accept the claims of both. A person consists of both good and bad attributes; to deny, therefore, part of oneself through an arbitrary moral code is to deny one's claim to the name *human being*. The argument is really between what might be called a "natural humanity" and an "artificial ideal." The ideal is artificial because it runs counter to natural inclination, and produces a contradiction in the personality that usually reveals itself in guilt or psychoneurosis. Zen serves to eliminate artificiality and to sweep away the psycho-ethical tensions that have marked the course of most Western philosophies. Life is restored to a natural harmony with the world; the staggering moral burdens of duty, honor, and "proper" conduct are seen as foreign accretions to the pure effortless simplicity of human existence. "In Buddhism," says T'ang master Lin-chi, "there is no place for using effort. Just be ordinary and nothing special. Eat your food, move your bowels, pass water, and when you're tired go and lie down. The ignorant will laugh at me, but the wise will understand."[14]

Such wise and ordinary effortlessness informs Ginsberg's technique of spontaneous writing (sometimes called "First thought, best thought")[15]: "The whole point of spontaneous improvisation in song is that you have to accept whatever thought presents itself to your rhyme—on the wing, so to speak. . . . You let your tongue go loose! . . . You can't change your mind—your mind is its own. And there's nothing heroic about that acceptance. . . . That's the whole point— it's ordinary mind!"[16]

Like Keats's "Negative Capability," which eschews all "irritable reaching after fact and reason," the spontaneous, "ordinary mind" (often with the assistance of drugs) relinquishes rational aloofness and reintegrates with the body and the world. "In 'Wales Visitation,' " Ginsberg reports, "I guess what I had come to was a realization that me making noise as poetry was no different from the wind making noise in the branches. It was just as natural. It was a *very important point.*"[17]

Whereas so much of traditional philosophy and theology stresses the disparity between humans and the natural world, Zen Buddhism offers the comfort of reintegration with nature. Material and spiritual boundaries are permitted to overlap; the conscious and the unconscious merge; an armistice is declared between ego and nature; and the satori experience—the awakening of an individual to a knowledge of his or her "inseparability" with the universe—is not a remote hope half-hidden in the shadows of eschatology but a very real, very immanent possibility.

Zen appealed to the beat personality in two other practical ways. First, it did not repress sexual feelings or activities. Sex was seen as a healthy, natural human instinct and was treated with respect and understanding. Second, its view of the inseparability of the universe precluded the stringent moralizing that characterizes Western religions. To be right was to follow one's natural bent; to be wrong was to resist instinct and to allow an artificial standard from outside the personality to govern one's life.

Zen submerges the ego into the "oneness" of the universe so that believers at no time consider themselves "something special" but rather as things among other things. The Zen follower, Alan Watts explains, views the ego as "his *persona* or social role, a somewhat arbitrary selection of experience with which he has been taught to identify himself. (Why, for example, do we say 'I think' but not 'I am beating my heart'?) Having seen this, he continues to play his social role without being taken in by it. He does not precipitately adopt a new role or play the role of having no role at all. He plays it cool."[18]

Beat Zen exaggerates two aspects of "pure" Zen: the holiness of the personal impulses and the idea of the Zen-lunatic or holy maniac. The sanctity of the spontaneous impulse justifies the principle of "spontaneous writing" as well as the characteristic confessional quality of beat literature. Art does not discriminate; every thought and feeling is sacred and thus appropriate for aesthetic registration.

The second aspect of beat Zen, the idea of the holy lunatic, is closely allied with the holiness of personal impulse. Such persons are revered because they deliberately confound the rational (artificial) tendencies of their disposition and therefore come closer to pure natural existence. Lunacy, in other words, is cultivated as a part of a long

discipline of disaffiliation from rational and material thought patterns. One deliberately deranges the senses that organize those patterns. Since LSD and narcotics are biochemical aids to this process of
deliberate derangement, their popularity among the beats is under-
standable.

Though Ginsberg unmistakably arose from a beat matrix, both
profiting and suffering from the media attention that was virtually
guaranteed, we should be alert to how he has over the years outgrown
many of its exaggerations and developed many of its positive orienta-
tions into a consistent and integrated life. Most markedly, he has
mellowed with age, transcending (through Buddhist meditation) the
chip-on-the-shoulder social protest stance that characterized his work
in the sixties, acknowledging, perhaps, Confucius's counsel that it is
better to be "human hearted than righteous."[19] When asked in 1976
how his meditation study changed his outlook on world politics,
Ginsberg replied: "It has changed it somewhat from a negative fix on
the 'fall of America' . . . into an appreciation of the fatal karmic flaws
in myself and the nation. Also with an attempt to make use of those
flaws or work with them—be aware of them—without animosity or
guilt; and find some basis for reconstruction of a humanly useful society, based mainly on a less attached, less apocalyptic view."[20] Review-
ing his life's work in 1984 for his *Collected Poems,* Ginsberg assessed
his sixties poetry as "politically obsessed, ephemeral, too much anger,
not enough family, not enough of my personal loves."[21]

Allen Ginsberg Himself

"Collected Poems," writes Ginsberg (in the "Author's Preface" to this
1984 compilation of his work) "may be read as a lifelong poem
including history, wherein things are symbols of themselves." As
with no other poet, Ginsberg's poems are his most comprehensive and
intimate biography. Little is left out. Still some chronological and
conceptual ordering of his life may help to complement and perhaps
"de-symbolize" some of the less than obvious events.

During his high school years in Paterson, Ginsberg remembers
thinking of himself "as a creep, a mystical creep. I had a good time,
was lonesome; but I first read Whitman there."[22] A Jewish, homosexual, raised in a household strangely presided over by a politically obsessed mother on the ragged fringes of sanity and an utterly straight

conventional father (himself a poet and high school teacher), Ginsberg inevitably felt himself the lonely outsider, a stance he assumed throughout his life and rendered symbolically in his poems through the figure of "the shrouded stranger."[23] He was seventeen years old when he entered Columbia as a prelaw student, following, as he tells us in *Kaddish*, his "high school mind hero, a jewish boy who became a doctor later" (*CP*, 214). Although he originally studied economics, joined the debating team, became editor of the *Columbia Review* and president of the Philolexian Society, he was most impressed with Lionel Trilling's great books seminar, which he took as a freshman. One of his classmates, Lucien Carr, encouraged him to write poetry, and he received further encouragement from Mark Van Doren. Two years later Ginsberg's friendship with Carr, who was involved in a fatal stabbing, was a contributing factor in Ginsberg's expulsion from the university. The actual charge was partly that Ginsberg wrote an obscenity on his dorm window,[24] but his main offense was being allegedly discovered in bed with Jack Kerouac, by Dean McKnight.

He moved to an off-campus apartment later shared by Kerouac and William Burroughs who, Ginsberg later claimed, "educated me more than Columbia, really."[25] Burroughs, thirteen years older than Ginsberg and later the author of the notorious satire *Naked Lunch*, was yet another mysterious "outsider" of the "shrouded stranger" mold who introduced Ginsberg to the subterranean Times Square world of drugs, gay bars, and crime. Kerouac, too, served as Ginsberg's tutor during this period, and the trio's apartment became a kind of beat salon, attracting a circle of friends including John Clellon Holmes, Lucien Carr, and eventually the mythical superhero and literary muse of the beat imagination, Neal Cassady.

Cassady, a product of Denver reform schools, was a "shrouded stranger" with flair, a supersensual, charismatic talker (immortalized as Dean Moriarty in Kerouac's *On the Road*), with whom Ginsberg immediately fell in love. They became sexual partners, but Ginsberg's passion was not equally reciprocated and the affair ended bitterly.[26] Even so, Cassady lived as a kind of mythic love-hero, even beyond his death in 1968, in Ginsberg's work and heart. The poem "Many Loves" (*CP*, 156–58) intimately documents the love affair, as does "The Green Automobile" (*CP*, 83–87) and the seventeen "Elegies for Neal Cassady" (*CP*, 487–508).[27]

Ginsberg returned to Columbia as an English major in the fall of 1946 after working at a variety of odd jobs and taking a four-month training course at the Merchant Marine Academy. After graduation from the academy he embarked on a seven-month voyage along the Atlantic and Gulf coasts, which probably gave him his first taste of adult nonacademic life.

Cassady had moved back to Denver, and in the spring of 1947 he wrote to Ginsberg of his compulsive need for him. As Harold Beaver puts it, Cassady "had a giant inferiority complex and was constantly afraid of letting Ginsberg slip as if (in his own words) he 'were a woman about to lose her man.' "[28] Ginsberg went to Denver only to find that Cassady had little time nor feeling for him. Ginsberg shipped out again on a freighter, the *John Blair,* to Africa via Marseilles for two months, making it impossible for him to register for fall classes at Columbia.

Throughout Ginsberg's stormy years at Columbia, the staid and traditional Lionel Trilling and Mark Van Doren respected and championed his unruly but brilliant promise, even though their young protégé was pursuing his own quite different interests in the literary underground. Diana Trilling described her husband's student as "middling tall, slight, dark, sallow; his dress suggested shabby gentility, poor brown tweed gone threadbare and yellow," but her maternal insight fixed on the pathos of his personal background: "His mother was in a mental institution, and she had been there, off and on, for a long time. This was the central and utterly persuasive fact of the young man's life. . . . Here was a boy on whom an outrageous unfairness had been perpetrated: his mother had fled from him into madness and now whoever crossed his path became somehow responsible, caught in the impossibility of rectifying what she had done."[29] The long moving elegy to his mother, *Kaddish,* substantiates her insight. A similar corroboration may be found in Ginsberg's observation: "I cut myself off from all women because I was afraid I'd discover my mother in them, or that I'd have the same problems with them that I had with her."[30]

After graduating in 1948, Ginsberg held a number of odd jobs: dishwasher at Bickford's Cafeteria, book reviewer for *Newsweek,* market research consultant, and reporter for a labor newspaper in Newark, a position he used as a pretext for meeting and interviewing the poet William Carlos Williams, who had a long and abiding prosodic influence on Ginsberg's work. Williams patiently read and criticized Ginsberg's early poems (particularly those collected in *The Gates of Wrath* and *Empty Mirror*), provided an introduction to *Howl,* and even included two of Ginsberg's personal letters in the fourth book of his epic *Paterson*.

In June of 1948, when his affair with Cassady (who had written of his marriage in April) had clearly ended, and when his mother's mental illness was growing worse, Ginsberg experienced the now legendary Blake vision that oriented the spiritual and vocational direction of his life for the next fifteen years. That same year, his friend Herbert Huncke (another criminally oriented "shrouded stranger" who had just been released from prison)[31] stored some stolen goods in Ginsberg's apartment. When, at Ginsberg's insistence, they removed the goods in a stolen car, they were arrested by the police. In lieu of prison, Ginsberg was sent to the New York State Psychiatric Institute for eight months where he met Carl Solomon, the dedicatee of *Howl*.

Solomon, the "lunatic saint" of *Howl*, introduced Ginsberg to the French surrealists and reinforced his sensitivity to the uses of literature as a political force. An outsider and antirationalist, Solomon was no doubt directly responsible for much of the rebellious rage against the system that erupted in *Howl*.

Ginsberg was released in the summer of 1949 and returned home to Paterson for several months. He visited Williams whose admiration and encouragement increased. Many of the poems in *The Gates of Wrath* and *Empty Mirror* reveal his fidelity to Williams's imagist and objectivist poetics.

After drifting back to Manhattan and supporting himself at various dead-end jobs, he journeyed to Mexico by way of Cuba in December of 1953 and, while exploring Mayan ruins, lived for six months as a guest on the *finca* of Karena Shields, an archaeologist and former actress who once played Jane in the Tarzan movies. It was here that he wrote the moving meditation "Siesta in Xbalba" (*CP*, 97).

Moving on to the San Francisco Bay area, he endured an uncomfortable reunion with Neal Cassady, who by this time had settled into a life of marriage and children; Ginsberg was once again reduced to amorous despair. He found employment in San Francisco as a marketing researcher and moved into an apartment with a girl friend. He quickly entered into San Francisco's literary scene and became acquainted with Kenneth Rexroth, Gary Snyder, Robert Duncan, Lawrence Ferlinghetti, and eventually Peter Orlovsky, who was to become his lifelong lover, friend, and spouse.[32] The most notable literary event of Ginsberg's San Francisco period was his now famous reading of the yet unpublished *Howl* at Six Gallery on 13 October 1955. The performance was electrifying and launched Ginsberg as a major poetic voice of the San Francisco Renaissance.

There was somewhat of a falling out between Ginsberg and the older San Francisco writers after this reading. Grudges and hurt feelings developed that troubled Ginsberg enough for him to ship out on a freighter for the Arctic and eventually return to New York. During the next few years he embarked on a series of travels: Tangier (to visit Burroughs), Spain, Italy, Vienna, Munich, Paris (where he wrote part four of *Kaddish*).

Naomi Ginsberg died at the Pilgrim State Mental Hospital on Long Island in 1956 and Allen completed his elegy to her, *Kaddish,* in 1959. In February 1960 he left for a writers' conference in Chile, which developed into six months of travel through Bolivia and the Peruvian Amazon in search of the hallucinogenic drug *yage,* a quest documented in the correspondence with William Burroughs published as *The Yage Letters.*[33] During this period he also experimented with several hallucinogens with Timothy Leary.[34]

By 1961 Ginsberg had become an internationally recognized poet and he once more traveled to France, Morocco, Greece, Israel, India, Vietnam, and Japan. In the Orient his commitment to Buddhist beliefs galvanized, an event documented in *Indian Journals: March 1962–May 1963* and in "The Change: *Kyoto-Tokyo Express*" (*CP,* 324). This was a decisive point in Ginsberg's spiritual development, for it marked his abandonment of the gods, devils, and angels that had haunted his visions since the Harlem Blake experience fifteen years before. It is important to acknowledge Ginsberg's spiritual shift here from a theistic Judeo-Christian to a nontheistic Buddhist base. Lewis Hyde reports Ginsberg's later reflection on this change: "at the time I believed in some sort of God and thus Angels, and religiousness— at present as Buddhist I see an awakened emptiness *(sûnyatâ)* as the crucial term. No God, no Self, not even Whitman's universal Self"[35] In 1972 Ginsberg made a formal commitment to the Buddhist faith.

Ginsberg suffered international political notoriety in 1965 when he was crowned *Kral Majales* (King of May) by the students of Prague and was subsequently expelled from Czechoslovakia by the authorities, who were alarmed and offended by his uninhibited behavior and political comments. Back in the United States he remained politically visible during the Democratic National Convention in Chicago in 1968. "Few people realized what a locked-up police state Chicago was," he recounted, "just like Prague."[36] But in Chicago, he was able to practice his Buddhist chanting techniques with practical success: "As a matter of fact, [the chanting] did stop a lot of violence; it really calmed several scenes where police didn't have remote-control orders to attack."[37]

In *Planet News* (1968) and *The Fall of America* (1972), written in a frenetic travelogue style, Ginsberg poetically crisscrosses the continent making taped descriptions on the run, which to Helen Vendler, at least, represent "the largest attempt since Whitman to encompass the enormous geographical and political reality of the United States."[38]

During the seventies and eighties, Ginsberg's media exposure has fallen off sharply. The times mellowed and, despite Ginsberg's demurral, he seems to have mellowed too. During summers, he receives instruction in meditation from his teacher Chögyam Trungpa and teaches himself at the Naropa Institute and the Jack Kerouac School of Disembodied Poetics, which he cofounded, in Boulder, Colorado.

Today, Ginsberg lives in modest style in his $260-a-month tenement apartment on the lower East Side of Manhattan. Although he lives penuriously (he owns no car, no television, buys his suits at the Salvation Army), he says he spends "$32,000 a year on secretaries, photocopying, printing photos, for travel, and for expenses for musicians who appear with him."[39] Peter Orlovsky, still his close friend, has moved out to live with Denise Mercedes and raise children.

"People ask me if I've gone respectable," he told an interviewer recently. "It's just the difference between reality and commercial imagery. These days it's a different stereotype. Before, I was disreputable; now I'm a yuppie. The stereotype used to be the rebel, the buffoon. Now it's the older man gone mellow, losing his inspiration."[40]

Much of his time and energy goes to fulfilling a $160,000 contract with Harper and Row for six volumes of his journals, letters, literary essays, lectures, and poems to be published within six years as a sequel to the 837-page *Collected Poems: 1947–1980.*

"Assembling the Collected Poems gave me the chance to see the whole spectrum of what I've been through," Ginsberg says. "I'm astounded and amazed at the thought." What did that whole spectrum teach? "My intention," he reports, "was to make a picture of my mind, mistakes and all. Of course, I learned I'm an idiot, a complete idiot who wasn't as prophetic as I thought I was. The crazy, angry philippic sometimes got in the way of clear perception." Poetically, he sounds today as though he has come full circle to a Buddhist ver-

sion of the Williams-like poetics with which he began: "[I] . . .
turned away from a theistic mind, using abstractions like 'the Infinite,' and toward a non-theistic, Buddhist concentration on seeing
what's there, paying attention to the thing itself." Politically, he feels
he made errors of judgment in his youth: "I thought the North Vietnamese would be a lot better than they've turned out to be and I
shouldn't have been marching against the shah of Iran because the
mullahs have turned out to be a lot worse."[41]

Chapter Two

From Beat to Buddha

In the "Author's Preface, Reader's Manual" to *Collected Poems: 1947–1980*, Allen Ginsberg records (under the rubric "Texture of Texts") the following words:

> "First thought, best thought." Spontaneous insight—the sequence of thought-forms passing naturally through ordinary mind—was always motif and method of these compositions.
>
> Syntax punctuation Capitalization remain idiosyncratic, retaining the variable measure of nervous systematics. In many poems, semi-irregular indentation of verse conforms to divisions of original notation or spacings of first thought-speech mindfully recollected. "Mind is shapely, Art is shapely."
>
> (*CP*, xx)

Remarkably, the work of thirty-three years, so this statement avers, has consistently cleaved to a poetics succinctly encompassed by two credos: "First thought, best thought" and "Mind is shapely, Art is shapely."

True, one can easily detect developments and apparent changes in style reading through this comprehensive collection, but after doing so, one is struck by how aptly these simple principles reveal the integrity underlying the otherwise bewildering accumulation of the Ginsberg canon.

The traditional tools of literary criticism that Ginsberg learned from Trilling and Van Doren at Columbia obviously miss the mark, but forty years have elapsed since then. Whitman, Pound, Williams, and Olson have emerged from the back streets of literary Bohemia to assume mainstream respectability, particularly in modern academic literary circles. The beat movement won a war of attrition with the establishment during the sixties with the result that so much of its then protestant attitude has been absorbed into the cultural fabric that today it is barely distinguishable from the norm. So-called beat themes—allegiance to spontaneity, rejection of artificial forms, commitment to physicality, pursuit of the nonmimetic—have generated a

15

poetics of their own with their own academically respectable theorists William Carlos Williams and Charles Olson. The poet-strikers of the fifties have become management in the eighties.

The matrix of Ginsberg's poetics is his understanding of William Blake's four "Zoas" or "classical divisions" of human nature:

There's reason, there's feeling, there's imagination and there's the body. If reason dominates the body and imagination and the heart, it becomes a tyrant. . . . If the heart tries to take over and push too far, then it becomes a parody of sentimental gush. If the imagination tries to take over and exclude reason and balance and proportion and body, you get some nutty LSD head, jumping naked in front of a car saying, 'Stop the machinery!' and getting run over. The body trying to take over, you get some musclebound jock. You have to have them all in balance.

Reason has become a 'horrific tyrant' in Western civilization and created the nuclear bomb which can destroy body, feeling and intimidate and all but destroy imagination.[1]

We may deduce from this and Ginsberg's remarks elsewhere, particularly his commitment to what he eventually labels "ordinary mind,"[2] that the major thrust of his poetry is to restore a salutary balance to the modern human experience by, if not deposing the "tyrant" reason, at least reducing it to parity.

In this respect, he seems to echo Charles Olson's lament that "we have lived long in a generalizing time, at least since 450 B.C. And it has had its effects on the best of men, on the best of things. Logos, or discourse, for example, has, in that time, so worked its abstractions into our concept and use of language that language's other function, speech, seems . . . in need of restoration."[3] For both Olson and Ginsberg, "discourse" is the legacy of "tyrant" reason and must be supplanted by speech. Whereas reason governs the "universe of discourse," exercising its authority through tradition and form; the authority that governs the "human universe" is spontaneous human experience. Thus, to quote Ginsberg, the poet must

> live
> in the physical world
>   moment to moment
> I must write down
>   every recurring thought
> stop every beating second.[4]

From this description of the poetic process, one conjures up the picture of the poet as a kind of divine recorder. William Burroughs, in fact, once put it this way: "There is only one thing a writer can write about: *what is in front of his senses at the moment of writing.* . . . I am a recording instrument. . . . I do not presume to impose 'story' 'plot' 'continuity.'"[5] The "physical world" is the writer's sounding board, and his heartbeat strikes against it so as to produce the recurring thought. The classical notion of the poet as maker seems quite beside the point here; what is suggested, rather, is the concept of the poet as diarist, an idea no doubt directly attributable to Walt Whitman. Just as predetermined form might impinge upon the authentic candor of a diary, so preconceived poetic form inhibits honesty, encourages affectation, and makes the poem referential to reality rather than reality itself. One is reminded of Whitman's lines in *Song of Myself*: "This hour I tell things in confidence, / I might not tell everybody, but I will tell you."[6] This is the technique of the confessional; the confessor willingly gives priority to the catharsis of thought and feeling over the structure that the catharsis itself is to discover. As A. R. Ammons understands the process:

The lines don't shape, predict, and limit whole-poem forms. . . . The reason is that external reality (time, place, event) dictates Ginsberg's means, so the means are outside the poem and, though unrecoverable, are more complete there. Certain things happened in a certain city at a certain time; a journal, or cata-travelog of accidentals. Opposite (for clarification) is the internal vision, selecting, transfiguring, making new and whole; the poet servant to the poem that exists apart in terms of its own reality. The unity in Ginsberg's work is Ginsberg in search of unity, so that the poems are fragments of the search.[7]

What Ammons describes is a poetic process that scarcely recognizes the existence of conventional form. No discursive authority impinges from outside the poem to adulterate or distort the purity of its experience. As Robert Duncan once sarcastically observed, "Form, to the mind obsessed by convention, is significant insofar as it shows control. What has no rime or reason is a bogie that must be dismissed from the horizons of the mind. . . . Wherever the feeling of control is lost, the feeling of form is lost."[8]

Any arbitrary attempt to intrude external control upon the fluid spontaneity of feeling is anathema to Ginsberg's view of literary creation. "What happens," he asks, if you make a distinction between what you tell your friends and what you tell your Muse? The problem is to break down that distinction: when you approach the Muse to talk as frankly as you would talk with yourself or with your friends . . . In other words . . . there should be no distinction between what we write down, and what we really know, to begin with. As we know it every day, with each other. And the hypocrisy of literature has been—you know like there's supposed to be a formal literature, which is supposed to be different from . . . in subject, in diction and even in organization, from our quotidian inspired lives.[9]

Form, for Ginsberg, is "never more than an extension of content."[10] Feeling, rhythm, religion, and drugs conspire to produce a vision that, by the brute force and honesty of its essence, bulldozes its way into poetic validity. The ingredients often achieve a quality of wholeness that cannot be fully appreciated by technical analysis alone. In short, it is not a question of art imitating nature for Ginsberg, but of art being nature.

But if reality consists of passionately felt interests germinating in a loosely controlled subjectivity (the dependence upon hallucinogens and narcotic stimulants would seem to mark Ginsberg's rejection of control), one cannot help muse a bit sadly on the priority that poetry has been assigned. One soon begins to suspect that poetry has been reduced to an avocation and that the real activity of the writer is a Faustian pursuit of larger and deeper truth, which threatens to take him out of the voice range of his audience. Poetry of this sort, which often resembles hasty communiqués sent back from the frontiers of inward exploration, perhaps deserves Karl Shapiro's censure that "poetry that defends fragmentation borders on apocalyptic knowledge and insane knowledge. Poetry that defends the derangement of the senses, synesthesia, associationalism and the like, drifts rapidly towards a religious state of mind in which poetry itself becomes a religion and an art of prophecy."[11]

Ginsberg seems often to confirm Shapiro's contention. On the issue of fragmentation, for instance, Ginsberg says that "I had the idea . . . that by the unexplainable, unexplained non-perspective line, that is, juxtaposition of one *word* against another, a *gap* between two words—like the space gap in the canvas—there'd be a gap between the two words which the mind would fill in with the sensation of existence. In other words when . . . Shakespeare says, 'In the dread vast' and 'middle.'"[12]

This defense of fragmentation through appeal to parataxis is not new; Erich Auerbach, who develops it at length in *Mimesis*, recognizes it as a technique for discrimination between reality and myth.[13] Myth, Auerbach contends, contains no paratactic gaps; it is self-contained in its own artificially constructed universe. The artist's control has filled in the gaps so that there are no intrusions seeping in from the "real world." Biblical language, he maintains, continually exhibits gaps; and paratactic gaps are what lift the Scriptures from myth and validate their reality.

Auerbach lends support to Shapiro's charge that "poetry that defends fragmentation borders on apocalyptic knowledge," and Ginsberg's self-avowed prophetic stance—not to mention his biblical rhetoric—suggests the same conclusion. Certainly, we hear the voice of the prophet in these lines from the end of part one of *Howl*: "the madman bum and angel beat in Time, unknown, yet putting down here what might be left to say in time come after death" (*CP*, 131).

Ginsberg defends fragmentation, it seems, for precisely the reasons Shapiro condemns it, underscoring perhaps that for Ginsberg poetry is a means to an end rather than an end in itself.

As early as his first contact with William Carlos Williams, Ginsberg began experimenting with ways to restore speech to the language of poetry. Williams, of course, advised him that "one active phrase is better than a whole page of inert writing because nobody will ever read or reread it, wheras the active phrase, even if it's not a complete sentence, is more interesting. Cut down to what's active."[14]

Williams was anticipating Olson's third dogma of "Projective Verse" that "ONE PERCEPTION MUST IMMEDIATELY AND DIRECTLY LEAD TO A FURTHER PERCEPTION."[15] *Howl*'s images obviously owe much to this counsel, but restoring speech to language entails more than just cutting down to what's active. Pure activity, Ginsberg recognizes, can only be achieved through the eradication of "self-consciousness." In the *Indian Journals* he declares that "the problem is to write Poetry . . . which *sounds* natural, not self conscious," defining literary self-consciousness as "simple 'sophomoric' recognizable egotistic self consciousness. . . . Not to be confused with awareness of process of language. . . . Not natural to the man in the man—merely a 'stance.'"[16]

Self-consciousness, then, is an attitude, a stance, that is hostile to the spontaneity that quickens the ordinary mind, and here Ginsberg shows his allegiance to "open form." Open form (sometimes called "composition by field," or "projective verse") is the epistemological effort of postmodernist poetics to become equal rather than referential to reality.[17] The writer follows no outside authority in creation but is wholly dominated during the creative act by the experience itself. This means, of course, that the pure reality of the experience cannot be adulterated by revision (the arbitrary intrusion of alien afterthought): "whatever you said at that moment was whatever you said at that moment," Ginsberg points out. "So in a sense you couldn't change, you could go on to another moment."[18]

The poem is not about a subject; it is the subject itself. It is unselfconscious because it is not separate from the experience it enacts and therefore cannot reflect upon it. It is performance rather than artifact.[19] By 1962 Ginsberg had moved in this subjective direction far enough to wonder, "how do you write poetry about poetry (not as objective abstract subject matter à la Robert Duncan or Pound)—but making use of a radical method eliminating subject matter altogether. . . . I seem to be delaying a step forward in this field (elimination of subject matter) and hanging on to habitual humanistic series of autobiographical photographs . . . although my own Consciousness has gone beyond the conceptual to the non-conceptual episodes of experience, inexpressible by old means of humanistic storytelling."[20] The burden for readers of such "open" work is that they find themselves "naked" in the poem's field. There is no conceptual apparatus, no formal tradition of "humanistic storytelling," to guide them. They are on their own. Since subject matter is inconsequential (ideally, even eliminated), "tyrant" reason famishes while the reader's body feasts on the physical energies of the poem. The images of such an "open" poem are not "autobiographical photographs"; rather, by virtue of the solidity that breath gives them, they are allowed the free play of their individual energies even while, through juxtaposition with other images, they create an energy field. Thus even images are for the body not the reason, and readers are expected to "avoid all irritable reaching after fact and reason" and to remain "in the absolute condition of present things," that is, in the energy field of the poem itself.[21]

In practice, open form boils down to Ginsberg talking.[22] Talk is a spontaneous, ongoing, irreversible, verbal act. The flexibility of conversational talk—its toleration of inconsistencies and logical imprecision—makes it an effective net for gathering particulars, even though this advantage may be bought at the expense of vagueness. But if there is no anterior subject matter, is vagueness, then, a liability?

Interestingly, the structure of nonwestern languages bears striking resemblance to English informal conversation. By way of accounting for a pervasive, annoying vagueness in the work of the Chinese philosopher Mencius he was attempting to translate, I. A. Richards was struck by how similar that "vagueness" seemed to

the successive attempts that a speaker will sometimes make to convey a thought which does not fit any ready formulation. He may intimate as he switches (with an "or rather" or a "perhaps I ought to say") over from one statement to another, that he is "developing" his thought. Those with a taste for clear, precise views (itself a result of special training) will accuse him of not knowing what he wants to say, or of having really no thought yet to utter. But there is another possibility—that a thought is present whose structure and content are not suited to available formulations, that these successive, perhaps incompatible, statements partly represent, partly misrepresent, an idea independent of them which none the less has its own order and coherent reference.[23]

Richard's observation describes Ginsberg's poetry to a very large extent; its form is an unusually supple mode immediately reflexive to the "condition of present things." It functions admirably "in uncertainties, Mysteries, doubts, without any irritable reaching after fact and reason." Can it be that the aggravation that traditionalists feel toward Ginsberg's "open" form is simply that it embarrasses them with the fact that our most meaningful experiences occur not in lofty elegies, majestic odes, or symmetrical sonnets but in the halting, inconsistent, difficulties, and proper confusions of people engaged in urgent talk?

Can we, though, seriously regard such conversation as art? What happens in talk? Is it mimetic activity? Does it hold up a mirror to nature, as Aristotle insisted art does? Or, if that claim seems irrelevant, can we hold that talk "improves" on nature, idealizing it? None of the classical critical approaches are relevant to Ginsberg's open forms, for they are mesmerized by the metaphor of artist-as-maker and art as the object-made. Talk, however, is an activity, a process, an event. True, it can be notated on the printed page, but its essential value is its movement. Its shifts, its false starts, its indecisions, its non sequiturs—these are participatory events that rise to art when, through heightened intensity and sense of collective experience, they become the requickening of a previous or anticipated emotion through rite, what the Greeks called *dromenon*, "the thing done."[24]

It is the "doing," the acting, that sets the value to Ginsberg's "talk." As Jane Harrison explains, "The Greeks had realized that to perform a rite you must *do* something, that is, you must not only feel something but express it in action, or, to put it psychologically, you must not only receive an impulse, you must react to it."[25] This kind of "doing" applies not only to the poet but to the reader as well. Talk is a social, collective activity. We may only nod our head occasionally, widen our eyes in surprise, grimace in exasperation, or simply sigh, but in urgent conversation we are called upon to "do," to react, to engage our energies with those of the poem.

Talk is particularly subversive to the prosodic authority of "tyrant" reason. When the young Ginsberg once asked Williams, "Why do you write almost-prose lines?" the good doctor replied: "Yesterday I heard a Polish laborer say, 'I'll kick yuh eye.' . . . How do you put that in iambic pentameter?" Ginsberg heard how the utterance had "a funny little rhythm all it's own" and suddenly realized that Williams "was hearing with raw ears."[26] It was William's "raw ear" that established the "lyric outburst" of the line as the rhythmic unit of his poetry,[27] a point amplified by Charles Olson: "the syllable is only the first child of the incest of verse. . . . The other child is the LINE. And together, these two, the syllable *and* the line, they make a poem. . . . And the line comes (I swear it) from the breath, from the breathing of the man who writes, at the moment that he writes, and thus is, it is here that, the daily work, the WORK, gets in, for only he, the man who writes, can declare, at every moment, the line its metric and its ending—where its breathing, shall come to, termination."[28]

Where Williams speaks of "lyric outburst" as the determiner of the line, Olson settles on breath; but the distinction is purely semantic, for Williams elsewhere has written: "We are reminded that the origin of our verse was the dance—and even if it had not been the dance, the heart when it is stirred has multiple beats, and verse at its most impassioned sets the heart violently to beating. But as the heart picks up we also begin to count. Finally, the measure for each language and environment is accepted. In English it is predominantly the iambic pentameter, but whether that is so for the language Whitman spoke is something else again."[29]

Olson and Williams make two points: one, that the basic constitu-
ent of the poem, the line, is not a product of "tyrant" reason but of
the body—either the breath or the heart; two, that it can be seen that
the form of language is not static but a function of place, time, and
emotion. The implications of these two premises form the basis for
Olson's theory of "Composition by Field":

Human Universe

> (1) The poem itself must, at all points, be a high energy-con-
> struct and, at all points, an energy discharge. . . .
>
> (2) FORM IS NEVER MORE THAN AN EXTENSION OF
> CONTENT. . . .
>
> (3) ONE PERCEPTION MUST IMMEDIATELY AND DIRECTLY LEAD
> TO A FURTHER PERCEPTION.[30]

Ginsberg's prosodic allegiance to these principles is manifest in his
earlier work. "Ideally," Ginsberg once said, "each line of *Howl* is a
single breath unit. . . . My breath is long—that's the Measure, one
physical-mental inspiration of thought contained in the elastic of a
breath." As an aside he added, "It probably bugs Williams now, but
it's a natural consequence, my own heightened conversation, not
cooler average-daily talk short breath. I got to mouth more madly
this way."[31]

The suggestion of apology in this last remark—the student justify-
ing his unruliness to a disapproving master—is an important clue to
understanding Ginsberg's unique style, which tends to soar above the
medial plane of a poetic theory that in principle he accepts. Ginsberg
wants to "mouth more madly." He feels, perhaps, a visionary need to
break through even the permissive, flexible control that Williams
deems essential. But when it comes to why he must do so, Ginsberg's
various replies seem deceptively flip: "Well, I got a longer breath
than Williams, or I'm Jewish, or I study yoga, or I sing long lines."[32]
Ginsberg does have a longer breath, he is Jewish, and he does study
yoga. He had to learn that he was Allen Ginsberg, not William Carlos Williams. "By 1955 I wrote poetry adapted from prose seeds,
journals, scratchings, arranged by phrasing or breath groups into little short-line patterns according to ideas of measure of American
speech I'd picked up from W. C. Williams' imagist preoccupations. I
suddenly turned aside in San Francisco, unemployment compensation

leisure, to follow my romantic inspiration—Hebraic-Melvillian bardic breath."[33]

The result was, of course, *Howl*; but one senses in Ginsberg's focus on breath a subtle loosening of his poetic allegiance to Williams's objectivist constraints. Breath, for Ginsberg, was not merely the delineator of the poetic line, it licensed his visionary and confessional mode. "Paying attention to the breath," he said, "wipes out that self-consciousness."[34]

The distinctive application of breath to his poetics opened Ginsberg to new creative influences that did not so much reject the teachings of Williams as show him possibilities beyond them. These influences would be difficult to catalogue comprehensively, but the principal one would seem to be Jack Kerouac.[35] Ginsberg's celebration of Kerouac can be found everywhere in the poetry and prose comments.[36]

A few excerpts from Kerouac's "Essentials of Spontaneous Prose" may serve to demonstrate his responsibility in luring Ginsberg beyond the limits of Williams's program. "Spontaneous Prose" itself draws heavily on Olson's principle that "ONE PERCEPTION MUST IMMEDIATELY AND DIRECTLY LEAD TO A FURTHER PERCEPTION": "No pause to think of a proper word but the infantile pileup of scatological build-up of words till satisfaction is gained, which will turn out to be a great appending rhythm to a thought and be in accordance with Great Law of Timing."[37]

The relevance of Kerouac's sanction of scatology to Ginsberg is easily discernible. Even sophisticated readers of Ginsberg's poetry are apt to be put off, perhaps bored by, his obsession not only with four-letter words, but with the clinical, strikingly nonerotic descriptions of his homosexuality. Kerouac's promotion of an "infantile pileup" of such features "till satisfaction is gained" suggests that the "pileup" is an exercise, aiming at the elimination of self-conscious inhibitions. Describing the genesis of *Howl*, for example, Ginsberg recalls, "I thought I wouldn't write a *poem* but just write what I wanted to without fear."[38] At that time Ginsberg still held that a poem was something separate from what he really felt and thought. He later experienced full scatological emancipation: "the beginning of the fear with me was, you know, what would my father say to something that I would write. At the time, writing *Howl*—for instance like I assumed when writing it that it was something that *could* not be published because I wouldn't want my daddy to see what was in there. . . . Though that disappeared as soon as the thing was real."[39]

Kerouac's phrase "No pause to think of proper word" is another technique for combatting self-consciousness. It is a device for neutralizing the discriminating intellect through sheer haste, thus attaining what Ginsberg later identified as "ordinary mind."[40]

We see the full dimensions of Kerouac's notion of "spontaneous" writing in his explanation of "Scoping": "Not 'selectivity' of expression but following free deviation (association of mind into limitless blow-on-subject seas of thought, swimming in sea of English with no discipline other than rhythms of rhetorical exhalation and expostulated statement. . . . Blow as deep as you want—write as deeply, fish as far down as you want, satisfy yourself first, then reader cannot fail to receive telepathic shock and meaning-excitement by same laws operating in his own human mind."[41] Both in terms of technique and rationale, Kerouac's words express the matrix of Ginsberg's abiding creative credo: "First thought, best thought" and "Mind is shapely, Art is shapely."

Although, there is nothing new in the concept of spontaneous creation (Plato recognized the sanctity of inspiration even while turning poets out of his republic, and the English Romantic poets zealously guarded each inspired comma), literary traditionalists have not been impressed by the reemergence of the notion. Annoyed by its subjective assumption that truth resides within, and reason can only corrupt the purity of truth's first gush, John Ciardi dubbed it "the holiness of the impromptu,"[42] but Alan Watts, generally a sympathetic reader of Ginsberg's work, raises the most telling criticism: "There is, indeed, a considerable therapeutic value in allowing oneself to be deeply aware of any sight or sound that may arise," he says. "But this is therapy; it is not yet art."[43] Ciardi seems to concur. Addressing Kerouac's opposition to revision on grounds that "whatever you try to delete . . . that's what's most interesting to a doctor," Ciardi concludes that the statement is "symptomatic of a narcissistic sickliness in all Beat writing. 'This is important,' it says, 'because it happened to sacred me.' The object seems to be to document one's own psyche on the assumption that every reader will find it as interesting as your psychiatrist does. Sorry, boys: I find it zany without illumination, precious rather than personal, and just plain dull."[44] Ginsberg's rejoinder to this—"Mind is shapely, Art is shapely"—is not likely to redeem his poetry from dullness for a traditionalist like Ciardi no matter how authentically free from artifice it may in fact be. But authenticity, as opposed to aesthetic merit, seems to be the criterion against which Ginsberg expects his poems to be measured—is the human experience that they communicate unselfconsciously real?

According to Francis Golffing and Barbara Gibbs, the poetic quest for unadulterated reality involves, for poets like Ginsberg, breaking down "the *logical* or *necessary* requirement of 'plot.'" Since plot is an artifice, it cannot be "life." A second technique they list is to make "the poem 'occasional' in a new sense—a 'throw away' rough jotting." The roughness presumable equates with "the real." Ginsberg's comment that *Howl* was composed without thought to publication suggests his relation to this principle. A third technique—one perhaps most relevant to Allen Ginsberg—is "luxuriating in the private and sensational at the expense of 'plot.' The poem might be conceived as as orgasm, or a series of orgasms, expressed in words like 'Wow,' 'Bomb,' and nonsense-syllables. sputterings, pseudo-puns (one where the second meaning has no relevance). The poet attempts to *do away* with the 'one remove,' the imitation. The poem becomes, or is meant to become, the experience itself."[45]

One might detect in this description a poetics that has lost faith in language, presumably because it is considered in thrall to "tyrant" reason. Authentic communication is possible only through words that "tend to be emotional explosions with no objective correlates."[46] On the positive side, one might see it as reflecting the emergence of apocalyptic poetry: not poetry about a thought or a feeling, but poetry as an event in itself. It is not difficult to understand why the claim is so often made that Ginsberg's poetry is unreadable. Ginsberg might be the first to agree; his poetry is not made to be read but to be lived through.

The Blake vision occupied Ginsberg's imagination through fifteen years of visionary expansion of consciousness during which he "actually believed that ordinary reality, sometime, could be replaced by the vastness of my vision of reality—a glimpse of a reality so brief that it seemed another mode."[47] It was eventually his India trip and commitment to Buddhism that, in a sense, brought him back full circle to his poetic beginnings with Williams: "Meeting a lot of holy men in India. Yeah, that changed me. You see, mainly getting over the fear of an absolute god outside of myself and coming to a slow realization that the divinity which was prophesied to me by Blake years ago was actually in myself rather than outside like a hidden god outside the universe . . . the change for me finally was a precipitation of my awareness back into my body from wandering in various alternative possible metaphysical universes experienced in visions or experienced under drugs."[48] Here is a new positive relationship with the material world that accepts the body, accepts the self, and, most interestingly, accepts the proper claims of rationality: "The idea that recognition of the body, recognition of Eros and recognition of sound would exclude rational intelligence is an error of judgment that only someone locked into hyper-rationalistic intelligence and nothing else, neither imagination nor body nor feeling, would make."[49]

Ginsberg's healthy, drugless return to the particularities of the world squares with Mark Shechner's opinion that "credit for Ginsberg's survival belongs to his Buddhism, which has taught him how to marshall and conserve his energies and to suspend his urban, Jewish agitation in passive, Eastern repose." It also squares with Shechner's further observation that "Ginsberg has kept faith with his earliest mentors—Williams, Whitman, and Blake."[50] Despite his rejection of the Blake experience and his obvious distancing from Williams's early imagist strictures, and despite his commitment to Buddhism, somehow Ginsberg has managed to forge a plausible coherence from these powerful influences that seems to work:

Now the Zen practice was paying complete absorbed attention to the immediate teapot and teacup in front of you and pouring the tea with complete absorption and intention, with the mind focused there observing every wavelet and droplet coming out of the spout into the teacup and then serving it with complete presence to the person in front of you. Blake's propositon was that "concrete particulars" were the essence of poetry and consciousness observation to see eternity, uh, no, "to seek all Heaven in a grain of sand, and eternity in an hour." Williams's proposition from American roots was: "so much depends / upon / a red wheel / barrow / glazed with rain / water / beside the white/chickens." When Williams said "so much depends," he means all human consciousness depends on direct observation of what's in front of you.[51]

There does seem to be an integrity to Ginsberg's poetics that remains fixed despite its many accretions—an integrity that should counterpoise Shechner's conclusion that "nothing he has done since the poems in *Kaddish* (1961) shows any advance in vision or technique."[52]

Chapter Three
The Gates of Wrath and *Empty Mirror*

The manuscript for *The Gates of Wrath* disappeared in the early fifties while being carried to London by a "lady friend." Ginsberg had no complete copy of it until 1968 when it was returned to him through Bob Dylan. Paul Christensen has described the collection as a "romantic encyclopedia of youthful emotions, all pitched into orthodox meters and rhymes."[1] Ginsberg's own "hindsight" seems to concur: the first two sonnets were inspired by Kerouac's *Town and the City*, he tells us (*CP*, 5), and the "poems hermetic" ("The Eye Altering" through "A Western Ballad" [*CP*, 7–13]) "refer to a breakthru of visionary consciousness 1948 [the Blake vision]." Blake's voice inspired the title for the volume, Ginsberg understanding that voice to instruct him to "annihilate" his "ordinary consciousness"[2] through mind expansion and "To find the Western path/ Right thro' the Gates of Wrath" (*CP*, 801).

There are experiments with bop rhythms, such as "Pull My Daisy" (*CP*, 24–25), but also the more somber poems developing the theme of the "Shrouded Stranger" (*CP*, 26), the "figure of dereliction" that, as John Ower puts it, "projects Ginsberg's sense of personal suffering, alienation, and rejection, of the sordidness of self and inner darkness."[3]

Many of the poems in *The Gates of Wrath*, such as "On Reading William Blake's 'The Sick Rose'" (*CP*, 6), "A Western Ballad" (*CP*, 13), "A Very Dove" (*CP*, 7), and "The Voice of Rock" (*CP*, 10), obsessively address the Blake vision. "Vision 1948," for example, seems a densely exploitive appropriation of seventeenth-century metaphysical trappings presumably to borrow traditional respectability for the experience. These visionary poems, larded as they are with pretentious formal artificiality, confirm Portugés's suspicion that Ginsberg was "trying to capture the 'visionary gleam' by copying the forms and styles of his mystic predecessors, such as Vaughan, St. John of the Cross, and others."[4]

Appended to *The Gates of Wrath* are four early undergraduate imitations of Marlowe, Marvell, Donne, and Hart Crane. These "Earlier" love poems were dedicated with uncharacteristic discretion to "N.C." with "love's gender . . . kept closet" (*CP*, 813).[5]

All in all, these early poems document the confused emotions and derivative modes of a fledgling poet who is feeling his way through a series of emotional and spiritual upheavals, a poet who has yet to find his own voice and who has had what he takes to be a cosmic visionary experience.

Shortly after his release from Rockland State Hospital Ginsberg sent nine of the poems in this collection to William Carlos Williams, who replied: "In this mode perfection is basic." He meant that if one insists upon. slavish acquiescence to conventional form, the only course is to acquiesce well. This tactful admonishment was enough to prompt Ginsberg's liberation from formalism and encourage his pursuit of the kind of spontaneity that Kerouac was then urging. "The poems were imperfect," Ginsberg acknowledged. "I responded by sending Williams several speedworthy notations that form the basis of book *Empty Mirror*, texts written roughly same years as these imperfect lyrics" (*CP*, 813).

The "speedworthy notations" apparently pleased Williams, for he wrote in his introduction to *Empty Mirror*: "A new sort of line, omitting memories of trees and watercourses and clouds and pleasant glades . . . exists today. It is measured by the passage of time without accent, monotonous, useless—unless you are drawn as Dante to see the truth, undressed, and to sway to a beat that . . . finds in the shuffling of human beings in all the stages of their day, the trip to the bathroom, to the stairs of the subway, the steps of office or factory routine the mystical measure of the passions" (*CP*, 809).

The poems in *Empty Mirror* were written between 1947 and 1952 and draw upon the same personal crises as *The Gates of Wrath*, but formally they demonstrate an important reorientation for Ginsberg along Williams's imagist lines. Ginsberg explains that he mixes the "imperfect literary rhymes" of *The Gates of Wrath* with the "raw-sketch practice poems" of *Empty Mirror* because "disparate simultaneous early styles juxtaposed aid recognition of grounded mode of writing encouraged by Dr. Williams, 'No ideas but in things'" (*CP*, xix).

The assurance that "Tonite all is well" that one encounters in the poem commemorating the "year of the iron birthday" (*CP*, 32) is immediately vitiated by the poet's resignation to a hopeless road ahead;

"What a terrible future," he sadly predicts. Ginsberg, twenty-three, regards the anniversary as a "gate of darkness."

Chronology is merely a metaphor in the context of this poem. The birthday is a convenient occasion for personal assessment, but the real subject is the poet's spiritual and emotional disrepair after the Blake experience and the "sudden termination of erotic spiritual, marriage mutually vowed" with Neal Cassady (*CP*, 813). The poet, "physically and/spiritually impotent" in the midst of a month of "madness," makes it quite clear that things cannot go on as they have. He awaits some "cue for passion" so that his life can proceed.

Ginsberg thought that Blake's voice was that cue urging him to withdraw from worldly concerns and pursue his "real" existence in the mind—to bifurcate living; that is, to ignore the body, as far as authentic existence is concerned, and to realize his destiny solely in the mind and in the spirit:

> I suddenly realized that my head
> is severed from my body;
> I realized it a few nights ago
> by myself
> lying sleepless on the couch.
>
> (*CP*, 32)

Here is a crude first step along the mystic way, a conclusion that gains support from the fact that the experience documented in this poem occurred after the Blake vision when Ginsberg had vowed: "this was what I was born for . . . never forget, never renig [*sic*], never deny. Never deny the voice—no, never *forget* it, don't get lost mentally wandering in other spirit worlds or American job worlds or advertising worlds or war worlds or earth worlds."[6]

The significance of this poem in terms of Ginsberg's literary development transcends by far its merit as poetry because it marks the beginning of a cycle starting with the Blake vision and ending on a Japanese train in 1963 when he wrote "The Change" (*CP*, 324). What transpired in the interim was a metaphysical journey in search of reality through various levels of consciousness outside the body. The direction of this search eventually took a dramatic turn after a series of conversations with holy men in India and with contemporary theologians such as Martin Buber. What Ginsberg learned from these conversations was that the vital area for seeking reality was within the self. As Ginsberg himself explains, the problem was "getting *in* the body rather than getting out of the human form.[7] Speaking of his talks with Buber, Ginsberg says: "I was thinking like loss of identity and confrontation with non-human universe as the main problem, and in a sense whether or not man had to evolve and change, and perhaps become non-human too. Melt into the universe, let us say. . . . Buber said that he was interested in man-to-man relationships, human-to-human."[8]

The severance of head from body in this very early poem is, therefore, a definite departure point that helps one navigate the tortuous course of Ginsberg's philosophical progress. For example, the consequence of a mind being haunted by visions is documented in "Psalm I":

The psalms are the workings of the vision haunted mind and not that reason
    which never changes.

I am flesh and blood, but my mind is the focus of much lightning.

I change with the weather, with the state of my finances, with the work I
    do, with my company.

But truly none of these is accountable for the majestic flaws of mind which
    have left my brain open to hallucination.

All work has been an imitation of the literary cackle in my head.

This gossip is an eccentric document to be lost in a library and rediscovered
    when the Dove descends.

                                                                    (*CP*, 18)

John Tytell sees this poem as one example of Ginsberg's legacy of surrealism, and formally this is true. The phrases "vision haunted mind" and "majestic flaws of mind," as Ginsberg employs them here, certainly do suggest modes by which "the total recovery of our psychic force by . . . the dizzying descent into ourselves"[9] may be achieved. The poem is also redolent with hermetic overtones, evident in several of the poems in *The Gates of Wrath*, such as "The Eye Altering Alters All" (*CP*, 7), which involve one's momentary awareness of the sacred resident in the profane world. "Psalm I" may be surreal, but first and foremost it is a religious poem couched in traditional religious idiom.

The style of the poem adapts to scriptural form by slackening from the tighter, more sparse type of verse seen in "Tonite all is well" (*CP*, 32). Its tension generates from the contrast in the first line between "vision haunted mind" and "reason which never changes." Oddly enough, the reason and the mind are opposites; a split in the mental process pits vision and spirit against the static, quantitative modus operandi of logic. Reason is the language of science—cold and uninspired; but "Mind," haunted, is the poet's openness to a sacred realm beyond the rigidity of cause and effect, employing a "negative capability," to use Keats's popular expression. Ginsberg's suspicion of reason is not based, therefore, upon a belief that humans are poor logicians but on the profounder conviction that they are something more than the best logician.

The word Ginsberg uses to suggest the supralogical dimension of the human mind is "flaws." "Flaws" are simply chinks in the rational armor through which one can make tentative forays into seemingly endless planes of nonrational reality. "My mind," Ginsberg says in this poem, "is the focus of much lightning," but what he means by *mind* is clearly not the ordinary denotation assigned to the term. Mind is not a mere receptor of knowledge but a focal point for visionary insight, and he seems to be deliberately insisting upon a distinction between the "mind" of line two and the "I" that opens line three. "I" is an ego on a lower cause-and-effect plane; it is subject to the vagaries of mood and meteorology. "I" am tired, the poet is saying; and so "I" can't think well today—a simple logical inference. But this "I," this rational ego, Ginsberg seems so eager to point out, is unreliable and has nothing to do with that part of a person that is above logical categories. This higher and more authentic nature finds syllogisms irrelevant and receives its knowledge of reality through the cracks in the imprisoning walls of logic. "Majestic flaws of the mind" are just that—majestic. They are portals to holiness.

The novelty of this conception for Ginsberg is reflected in the next line where he suggests that his previous work has not followed this inspiration. It has been derivative: "an imitation of the literary cackle in my head." "Psalm I," however, is of a new order. It is "gossip," yes, but gossip about nocturnal trysts with reality, which will mean little to readers until they too come to understand that humans are more than the best logician "when the Dove descends." Both the prophet and the egotist appear to haunt these lines, but so too does the spirit of a man who is convinced he has grasped something timeless. "The thing I understood from Blake," Ginsberg explains, "was that it is possible to transmit a message through time which could reach the enlightened, that poetry had a definite effect, it wasn't just pretty, or just beautiful, as I had understood pretty beauty before—it was something basic to human existence, or it reached something, it reached the bottom of human existence."[10]

"Cézanne's Ports" (*CP*, 53) was undoubtedly written with the intention of exciting its readers' "majestic flaws of mind." Although it seems to owe something to William Carlos Williams's much-anthologized "The Yachts," the poem reflects Ginsberg's fascination with Cézanne's attempts to trick the mind out of its customary patterns of reception. What Cézanne hoped to achieve with plastic, visual effects, Ginsberg aspired to accomplish with words. According to the French painter, the technique was to discover or recover what he termed "*petites sensations.*" Paul Tillich, also an admirer of Cézanne's canvases, has described the procedure as an artistic treatment of unorganic cubic forms in such a way that "the power of being itself" becomes embodied in them. It is, he continues, "nothing else than an attempt to look into the depths of reality, below . . . any beautification of the surface."[11]

Ginsberg's "majestic flaws of mind" (or what he in some cases calls "gaps") are the equivalents of Cézanne's *petites sensations* and indeed are intended to be glimpses "into the depths of reality." Close study of the two-dimensional surfaces of Cézanne's paintings, Ginsberg discovered, caused them to flash into three-dimensional space objects.[12] As he squinted at the pictures, three-dimensional "openings" occurred, not unlike the cosmic sensations he had experienced in the Blake visions. When he experimented with the phenomenon under the influence of marijuana, he came to the conclusion that Cézanne was reconstituting not physical objects into cubist forms, but rather his own ocular impressions of those forms. Cézanne was, in effect, observing his eyes observing a scene. Ginsberg suddenly realized that the artist's focus of attention was not outward, toward the object, but inward, toward the impression that the object had made upon his consciousness. It was, in fact, a phenomenological posture; reality was not objective stuff "out there"; it was inward phenomena, inward experience.

The acknowledgment of reality as an inward experience apprehended through *petites sensations* or "majestic flaws of mind" is crucial to Ginsberg's conviction of the holiness of everything. "Majestic

flaws" are nonconceptual flashes of sacred understanding or, as Cézanne confidently proclaimed, "nothing other than *pater omnipotens aeterna deus.*"[13]

The artist's obligation within this context is to create situations
where the *pater omnipotens* can speak. The poet or painter must cause
breaks in the rational continuity of existence through the uncovering
of "flaws" that in turn produce *petites sensations.* In painting, *petites sensations* are achieved through striking juxtapositions of geometric
masses; in religious language they are gained by similarly "odd" juxtapositions of worldly "models" with theological "qualifiers."[14] Ginsberg's "majestic flaws" are similiarly constructed, so that through
their "irrational" yoking of disparate words and images they disrupt
the authority of reason and allow "holiness" to enter. Ginsberg has
said that "one can see through [Cézanne's] canvas to God."[15]

As a poem, "Cézanne's Ports" pales before the theory behind it.
The cosmic allegory seems painfully strained, particularly when one
considers that it was taken secondhand from the painting; for example: "In the foreground we see time and life swept in a race," and
"the other side of the bay / is Heaven and Eternity." Part of Ginsberg's appreciation of this particular painting can be explained by its
Eastern mode of centering upon what is not included within the
frame. Ginsberg notes, for instance, that the "meeting place" of the
shores (Heaven, Eternity) "doesn't occur on the canvas" and that there
is "a bleak white haze over its mountains." Such interest in the non-
represented is patently mystical, but one feels that looking through
this particular glass darkly makes for a blurry poetic experience.

"After All, What Else Is There to Say" (*CP*, 29) attempts much
less than "Cézanne's Ports." This poem about the writing of poetry
implies the question "What is the function of poetry?" The answer in
the last line is "telling the truth." Between the question and the answer runs one word of pungent, practical advice from Ginsberg on
how to achieve the truth: "Wait." Waiting is the writer's strategy for
breaking though the veil in order to see the "universe itself." The
veil, in this case, is the poet's own mind which "turns / in a kind of
feminine madness of chatter." Chatter, like radio static that interferes
with communication, recalls "the literary cackle in my head" mentioned in "Psalm I" (*CP*, 18). "Chatter" and "cackle" are obstacles to
"telling the truth" because they are the residue of secondhand ideas
that clog the channels of pure inspiration. The only way to clear these
channels is through sheer patience—waiting. The poet must wait un-

til the scratchy static of the impure immediate response subsides before the scene can speak for itself—before "the sky / appears as it is."

In terms of poetic theory, "After All, What Else Is There to Say" is a case study of how Olson's projective principle ("FORM IS NEVER MORE THAN AN EXTENSION OF CONTENT") is actually put to work. "Chatter" and "cackle" (probably what Olson meant by "the lyrical interference of the ego") are symptoms of the poet's subversive attempt to impose an alien order upon material. The impulse must be allowed to die before the poem can come into being with fidelity; "emotion," as Wordsworth knew, should be poetically "recollected in tranquility":

> I wait: wait till the sky
>   appears as it is,
> wait for a moment when
>   the poem itself
> is my way of speaking out, not
> declaiming of celebrating, yet,
>   but telling the truth.
>   (*CP*, 29)

The title of the poem provides the text against which the description of the creative problem is held in evidence. There is nothing else to say, save "*what is in front of . . . [*the poet's] *senses at the moment of writing.*" William Burroughs, the articulator of this conviction, mirrors Ginsberg's position precisely by adding that, as a poet, "I am a recording instrument . . . I do not presume to impose 'story' 'plot' 'continuity.'"[16]

"Fyodor" (*CP*, 32) is an interesting exercise in the subtleties of naming. The names one uses for objects and people can be seen as indices to one's feelings toward them, and Ginsberg exploits this human propensity with technical brilliance in this short account of his impressions of Dostoyevsky. Whatever profundity is to be found in this poem is contained in its implicit insistence that the "reality" of Fyodor is not inherent in the Russian novelist himself but lies in the impressions of Dostoyevsky that exist in Ginsberg's growing consciousness of him—a phenomenological theory similar to that expressed vis-à-vis Cézanne.

The various names Ginsberg uses for his Russian subject are the technical media through which he communicates the "reality" of Fyodor at various stages of his experience of him. The first impression, for example, is one of unfamiliarity: "My original version of D. / before I read him. . . ." This powerful but as yet unfamiliar acquaintance is characterized by the empty, inconclusive abbreviation "D." Later Fyodor seems to peer into Ginsberg's consciousness with the mystic inprecision of awe: "The death's head of realism," "the dark / haunted-house man, wild, aged, / spectral Russian." When Fyodor becomes an imposing force—mysterious and alien—this impression is reflected in the alien spelling of his name: "Dostoievski." Eventually, Fyodor is read and understood: "realities coincide, and it is discovered that they are brothers under the skin. "I call him Dusty now, Ginsberg says with American camaraderie, although he acknowledges his lack of exclusive franchise by adding: "but he is Dostoyevsky" [American spelling]. The personal illumination of the poem is the poet's admiration of his own prophetic talent even as a child. It is as if to say, "I just knew I'd like Dostoievski even though I've barely heard of him."

Very often in what is called emblem poetry a physical description is rendered that is wrenched into significance by a seemingly unrelated title. George Herbert's "The Pulley" is a good example, or Ginsberg's own "The Eye Altering Alters All" (*CP*, 7). This technique is often associated with paintings in which the artist demands that the viewer "not accept the surface alone" but penetrate "into those depths in which the tension of the forces creates nature."[17] In poetry, the title often serves as a trap door through which the reader plummets to a deeper understanding of what is inherent in the picture rendered. One of Ginsberg's early experiments with this technique is "The Trembling of the Veil" (*CP*, 14), which, while it evokes Ginsberg's visionary experience of an otherwise natural scene, exhibits Williams's quiet objectivist influence.

Two phrases in this deceptively simple, natural, descriptive poem show how Ginsberg's surrealistic vision causes him to deviate from the classic methodology of Williams and also point to a characteristic problem in much of Ginsberg's verse. The phrases are similes: (1) the trees "like live organisms on the moon," and (2) the bough "like a hairy protuberance." If this were merely a descriptive nature poem, then one might expect it in principle to "render" the scene by avoiding metaphor and simile (following Williams's credo of "no ideas but in things"). The meaning of the poem should emerge from its structure and not from some heavyhanded authorial intrusion. Viewed as a "nature" poem, it would be difficult to defend its similes because they draw attention away from the immediacy of the natural scene. In fact, one could argue, the similes weaken the poem's climactic *petite sensation* by disclosing it in advance. The similes, in other words, are leaks through which the kinetic energy of the poem prematurely drains. What is the purpose of seeing the trees as lunar "organisms" when the structure of the poem depends upon the reader's acknowledgment that they are distinctly natural earthly phenomena? Why must the bough be "hairy" (introducing a confusion between flora and fauna) when it is precisely the botanical essence of the tree that the structural energy of the poem requires? The answers to these questions, which the poem's title anticipates, is that the scene we are made privy to is not "nature" at all but "vision"—a vision in which the trees *are* "lunar organisms" and the boughs *are* "hairy."[18] The poet here is not making a poem; he describes what he in fact sees. The result is thus too naive in conception to bear the weight of sophisticated explication.

A less ingenuous Ginsberg might have said to himself, "What Else is There to Say?" and simply crafted his poem, as Williams would advise, so that his visionary experience might be evoked through his arrangement of "natural" objects. But this would be referential to the vision of the poem's reality, not the reality of the vision itself. This perhaps explains why reviewers seem to exaggerate a tension they sense between Ginsberg and Williams on the matter of form. Robert Hazel, for example, when he reviewed *Empty Mirror* for the *Nation*, wrote: "These early poems are a development of the anti-poetic principle of Williams, but Ginsberg is not subservient to Williams; he does not, like Williams, carefully keep the voice down, but to a considerable degree restores elements of Cranian rhetoric to the Williams canon."[19] Ginsberg is not insensitive to the limitations of poetry in fully evoking mystic visions:

> I attempted to concentrate
> the total sun's rays in
> each poem as through a glass,
> but such magnification
> did not set the page on fire.
>
> (*CP*, 33)

In the "Bricklayer's Lunch Hour," which bears a superficial similarity to "The Trembling of the Veil" in form and intention, Ginsberg does "carefully keep the voice down"; and the absence of rhetoric does much toward fulfilling Williams's counsel that "the writing cannot be made to be 'a kind of prose,' not prose with a dirty wash of a stale poem over it"; and also that "it must not set out, as poets are taught or have a tendency to do, to deceive, to sneak over a poetic way of laying down phrases" (*CP*, 810). The poem is extraordinarily Williamsesque, earning by that quality even Marianne Moore's grudging approbation.[20] Perhaps the reason is the poem's occasion, which, unlike "The Trembling of the Veil," has nothing to do with vision, but more likely with anticipation of amorous disappointment. It was originally a journal notation Ginsberg made in Denver while waiting for Neal Cassady to return from work, and its threatening ending—

> Meanwhile it is darkening as if to rain
> and the wind on top of the trees in the
> street comes through almost harshly.
>
> (*CP*, 4)

—likely portends romantic disappointment rather than the cosmic vision evoked by the images in "The Trembling of the Veil."

Barely qualifying as a vignette, the poem structurally matches the commonplaces of the scene with a spare, matter-of-fact treatment. The language is the good, unsmeared American idiom favored by Williams, unpretentious and carefully calculated to catch the monotony of an unexceptional workday. The effect of the poem depends upon "framing" the inconsequential in order to expose an inherent significance that would otherwise be lost outside the poetic medium. The framing is accomplished by the trivial but essentially human gesture of the laborer placing his hat over a kitten's body, coupled with suggestions of imminent catastrophe: the darkening of the sky and the sudden, harsh wind. The trick of this poem is the way in which Ginsberg manages to deepen the surface of the workaday scene, how he effects the extraordinary in the ordinary. But, as Marianne Moore discerned, the trick has Williams's patent on it.

When Ginsberg experienced his Blake vision in a New York tenement, he crawled out on a fire escape, rapped on the window of a neighboring apartment, and screamed, "I have seen God!"[21] He often refers to God in his early poetry, but the precise character of his deity is usually clouded in ambiguity. When Blake spoke to him, "It was like God had a human voice. . . . Or that God was in front of my eyes—existence itself was God."[22] The general impression one gets is that "God" is an imminent kind of depth-dimension who is accessible through "cosmic consciousness." His residence is definitely in this world because cosmic consciousness reveals "all of heaven in a flower. Or what was it—eternity in a flower . . . heaven in a grain of sand?"[23] "The world is holy! . . . Everyman's an angel!" (*CP*, 134). Cosmic consciousness confirms that there is but one world and it is absolute, holy and eternal:

> This is the one and only
> firmament; therefore
> it is the absolute world.
> There is no other world.
> The circle is complete.
> I am living in Eternity.
> The ways of this world
> are the ways of Heaven.
>   (*CP*, 33)

The equation could not be simpler: the world equals eternity; worldly existence is the only one human beings will ever know.

Despite the apparent holiness of all human experience, God also appeared to Ginsberg in frightening forms: "like real serpent-fear entering the sky . . . like the hand of death coming down on me—some really scary presence." Just as the Judeo-Christian God reveals both a wrathful and a comforting aspect, so did Ginsberg's cosmic awareness have its light and dark sides, but the sacred importance was the breakthrough itself, which apparently could take the form of ecstatic rebirth or terrifying death: "it was almost as if I saw God again except God was the devil. The consciousness of itself was *so* vast, much more vast than any idea of it I'd had or any experience I'd had, that it was not even human anymore—and was in a sense a threat, because I was going to die into that inhuman ultimately. I don't know *what* the score was there—I was too cowardly to pursue it. . . . I shut it all off. And got scared, and thought, I've gone too far."[24] Even so, Ginsberg's death theme, particularly his fear of death, is a "major motif" in his poems through to "The Change," all of them exploring death, as Portugés notes, "as a means of altering consciousness and of achieving the break-through into Eternity."[25]

"In Death, Cannot Reach What is Most Near" opens with what appears to be a conundrum:

> We know all about death that
> we will ever know because
> we have all experienced
> the state before birth.
>
> (CP, 34)

Because there is no cognition before birth, one might assume that we know nothing of death. But if the world is absolute, holy, and eternal, death is simply a name for one state of being in that world. People may in life be imprisoned in "self-consciousness," but in death find a liberation to eternal, "cosmic consciousness." Ginsberg quickens this notion with a subtle borrowing of the famous metaphor from the Venerable Bede:

> Life seems a passage between
> two doors to the darkness.
> Both are the same and truly
> eternal and perhaps it may
> be said that we meet in
> darkness. The nature of time
> is illuminated by this
> meeting of eternal ends.
>
> (CP, 34)

The meaning here is obscure, but some light might be shed on "the nature of time" and death by reference to Ginsberg's reminiscence, after his commitment to Buddhism, of his thinking at that time:

I actually believed that ordinary reality, sometime could be replaced by the vastness of my vision reality—a glimpse of a reality so brief that it seemed another mode. But, maybe ordinary consciousness slowly encompasses death—in a very subtle way, a very slow, creeping way. It might even be like the renunciation of nirvana, which is an idea, which is the original perception of samsara and nirvana—or time and eternity. The terms become identical Time is eternity, eternity is time. . . . I wasn't smart enough to think of that formula. That is why I like Buddhism, because Buddhism does provide the mental formulas for recognizing and categorizing that kind of experience.[26]

Actually, Ginsberg was "smart enough to think of that formula," as the final stanza of the poem clearly shows:

> It is amazing to think that
> thought and personality
> of man is perpetuated in
> time after his passage
> to eternity. And one time
> is all Time if you look
> at it out of the grave.
>
> (*CP*, 34)

Perhaps the notion was not so much an anticipation of Buddhist thought as a recollection of Walt Whitman's, who wrote in *Song of Myself*:

> . . . I accept Time absolutely,
> It alone is without flaw, it alone rounds and completes all,
> That mystic baffling wonder alone completes all.[27]

The fact that "all Time" and "one time" become the same from the viewpoint of the grave assures one that an honest acknowledgment of death is also an honest acceptance of life.

"This is about death" is another of those emblem poems whose title injects a significance that otherwise would not be there. "Being" is what the universe shouts, and all art and thought must return to that source, which the title instructs is death. Only the consoling formula that time is eternity from the vantage point of the grave saves the poem from nihilism.

"The Terms in Which I Think of Reality" (*CP*, 50–51) is a tripartite sociophilosophical sounding of Ginsberg's dialogue with the world. The first stanza rather neatly links this effort with the three previous ventures into philosophy with an insistence upon the finiteness of the human ontological predicament:

> Reality is a question
> of realizing how real
> the world is already.

The stanza promises a program of a demythologization and carries through with a series of premises already implied in the previous poems: "Time is Eternity," "everyone's an angel," and the like. The

equation of time with eternity is a paradoxical assertion that sup-
plants objective time-keeping with subjective time-living. The according of angelic status to all is not flattery but a hopeful conviction
that people are indeed angels under their thick skins of hypocrisy.
The new element introduced in this poem is the idea that reality is
"Heaven's mystery / of changing perfection." Eternity (which is time)
is not an absolute; in fact, "absolutely Eternity / changes!" Evidence?
"Cars are always / going down the street, / lamps go off and on."
People live in Eternity. Eternity is real. Reality changes.

All that is left to complete this first section is a moral judgment,
and it comes in aesthetic clothing: "The motion / of change is beautiful, as well as form called / in and out of being." Change (death being the supreme mutation) is nature's secret source of beauty, and the
first part of the poem ends on that note. As a statement of position,
this section perhaps suffices. As poetry, however, it is not much more
than a metaphysician's hasty outline of Wallace Stevens's "Sunday
Morning." Ginsberg is clearly out of his metiér.

Phase two of the poem puts theory into practice or, as Ginsberg
rather verbosely puts it,

> . . . to distinguish process
> in its particularity with
> an eye to the initiation
>
> of gratifying new changes
> desired in the real world.
> (CP, 50)

This language is simply indefensible as prose, poetry, or even satire.
Wallace Stevens knew how to poke fun at pedagoguery:

> Nota: man is the intelligence of his soul,
> The sovereign ghost. As such, the Socrates
> Of snails, musician of pears, principium
> And Lex.[28]

Ginsberg is not poking fun; or, if he is, he has no talent for it.
Neither is he speaking (as Williams claims in the Introduction that
he should) "in plain terms, such as men will recognize" (CP, 809).
The intent here is not to compare Ginsberg to Stevens, but merely to

point out that Ginsberg has allowed himself to become derailed from his natural track.[29] What he wants to say is simply that the present world is full of unpleasantness, and the only way one can improve it is by bits and pieces. The practical movement of the poet's intention is blunted and deformed by a sophomoric pseudorhetoric.

Part three of the poem abandons the previous method and deals with the universal human situation in a less-than-perfect world. The medium is an extended metaphor in which humanity is likened to "the unhappy / whore on River Street," and its sad plight is unraveled in the idiom of prostitution. Thus, the oldest dilemma in the world is presented in terms of the oldest profession. The search for love is rewarded with "snide remarks" and "a couple of bucks." Even worse, the poor whore, humanity, has

> never really heard of a glad
> job or joyous marriage or
> a difference in the heart:
> or thinks it isn't for her,
> which is her worst misery.

The theorized reality of part one is unknown to the factual reality of part three. The chasm that separates the two constitutes the greatest tragedy of all.

Scattered throughout *Empty Mirror* are poems that fall roughly under the heading of dream allegories. Narrative in structure, they generally center on some aspect of social sickness that Ginsberg usually sees in terms of a man thrown into a Kafkaesque situation of meaninglessness and finding no way nor no one with whom to communicate, "A Crazy Spiritual" (*CP*, 75) is one example; "Two Boys Went into a Dream Diner" (*CP*, 55), another. Some have a semihumorous yet ironic twist to them, such as "How Come He Got Canned at the Ribbon Factory" (*CP*, 60) or "The Archetype Poem" (*CP*, 61). Typical is "A Meaningless Institution" (*CP*, 15).

The "enormous ward" in which the protagonist of the poem is thrust dramatizes the Ginsberg-Heidegger analysis of existence in which humanity is called upon to acknowledge its ignorance of the "whence and whither" and to skirmish as best as possible in an apparently irrational world. The ward is deliberately reminiscent of a military barracks, and the narrator is issued "bedding, and a bunk . . .

surrounded by hundreds of weeping, / decaying men and women."
From a vantage point "three tiers up," he enjoys an overview of the
world—similar to scenes from *Piers Plowman*—that reveals "gray
aisles," "Old, crippled, dumb people," and "a heavy girl / in a dirty
dress" who stares at him. The feeling of paralysis that the description
engenders seems to derive from a total absence of communication.
There is no one to explain, no one to advise. He waits, incommuni-
cado "for an official guide to come / and give me instructions"; but,
of course, there is none. The denouement is an archetypical catastrophe of meaninglessness:

> After awhile, I wandered
> off down empty corridors
> in search of a toilet.[30]

This theme is the classic one of the twentieth century. Ginsberg's
forlorn hero, just another confused mute "waiting for Godot," finally
gives up his senseless vigil for a cosmic guide and attends to the practical necessities of animal nature. The moral is suggestively anchored
in the title: "A Meaningless Institution." The two nouns irrevocably
correspond; all institutions are meaningless, and the human tragedy
is that humanity has forfeited its birthright by institutionalizing its
existence.

Is there any way out of such a predicament? One exit sign flickers
dimly in the poem "In Society" (*CP*, 3). In this "dream,"[31] written
a year before "A Meaningless Institution," one finds an almost identical form and theme; only the scene had been changed. The poem
moves us from a ward to a cocktail party. Toward the end of the
poem, the narrator is rebuffed by a "fluffy female who looked like / a
princess." She glares at the hero, says, "I don't like you," and turns
her head away, refusing to be introduced. The allegory is fairly explicit: it is a case of perverse refusal to communicate with an implicit
suggestion that the "princess" has forgotten (or never known) that she
is really an "angel."

Her rudeness initiates an explosive reaction: "Why you shit-faced
fool! . . . . Why you narcissistic bitch! How / can you decide when
you don't even / know me." The hero shouts his presence into the
room, communicating to an incommunicable world in the only way
possible—sheer vatic blitzkrieg:

> I continued in a violent
> and messianic voice, inspired at
> last, dominating the whole room.
>
> (*CP*, 3)

A "messianic voice" is the only one possible, the poem suggests, in a world that doesn't listen and behaves like a "narcissistic bitch." It is a shout that in eight years would crescendo into a howl.[32]

Some of the best poetry in *Empty Mirror* is the least pretentious and the most indebted to Williams if for no other reason than it deals with "the literal *things* of an immediate environment." These poems require no explanation, only acknowledgment and appreciation. They include such verses as the bleak "Sunset" with its opening lines:

> The whole blear world
> of smoke and twisted steel
> around my head in a railroad
> car. . . . (*CP*, 37)

or "A Ghost May Come" (*CP*, 71) with its simple haunting catalogue of "human beings in all the stages of their day" (*CP*, 809).

In *The Gates of Wrath*, the mythical derelict of "The Shrouded Stranger" graphically depicts the nature of Ginsberg's "outsider" motif:

> My flesh is cinder my face is snow
> I walk the railroad to and fro
> When city streets are black and dead
> The railroad embankment is my bed.
>
> (*CP*, 26)

This symbol of all that society rejects seeks lover-recruits:

> Who'll come lie down in the dark with me
> Belly to belly and knee to knee
> Who'll look into my hooded eye
> Who'll lie down under my darkened thigh?

Our viewpoint changes in *Empty Mirror*'s "Shrouded Stranger" (*CP*, 47); here we look at "the old bastard" from an exterior perspective

("Abhorred he sits upon the city dump. / His broken heart's a bag of shit") and introduce a persona in quest of this symbolic outcast: "I dreamed I . . . decided to go down the years / Looking for the Shrouded Stranger." The theme is simple enough—the sorry cast-off state of human feelings in a materialistic culture—and there is potential irony in the climax when the quester fails to recognize his grail and is told: "I'll bet you didn't think / it was me after all" (CP, 48), but the would-be profundity in this poem is too strenuously induced. Even Ginsberg, by the time he gets to the fourth section, seems to apologize:

> . . . it
> was going to tell a story;
> it was to be a mass of images
> moving on a page, with
> a hollow voice at the center.

Of all the poems in *Empty Mirror*, three in particular provide the most reliable preview of coming attractions: "Psalm I," "Hymn," and "Paterson." All three represent quests for a "hip" version of the beatific vision, and it is not accidental that they should all avail themselves of essentially religious symbol and form. "Psalm I" sets the pattern for the other two with its insistence upon the separation between "the vision haunted Mind" and "that reason which never changes" (CP, 18). The psalm places absolute trust in "the majestic flaws of mind" and introduces a prophetic theme by implying that "this gossip" will be "lost in a library and rediscovered when the Dove descends." It is an antirationalist poem that expresses Ginsberg's ubiquitous Blake theme that "tyrant" reason, if unchecked, disenfranchises the imagination, the heart, and the body.

"Hymn" (CP, 36) is the best preview of Ginsberg's future work. It is structured in lines that are superlyrical "take-offs"—the same "gone dithyrambs" that give *Howl* its mesmerizing power. "Hymn," however, for all its technical anticipation of *Howl*, strives for apocalyptic evocation but flounders into muddy vagueness. The usual themes are there: mortality ("this clock of meat bleakly pining for its sweet immaterial paradise"); "cosmic consciousness" ("the mind's angelical empyrean which shall . . . come to be known as the clock of light"); and a passionate aspiration for mystic vision that underscores an extreme disillusionment with the world as it is.

A mystic "otherworldliness" saturating this poem clashes with Ginsberg's other religio-philosophic expressions that, while apocalyptic in tone, are not essentially transcendental. Thus, "Hymn" generates some theological confusion. The apparent yearning for "immaterial paradise" and the overt eschatological symbolism of the final stanza ("the final gate," "the Diamond Seraph with 3 forks of lightning 7 claps of thunder," etc.) clash with the persistent equation of time and eternity and the constant, implicit suggestion that the only heaven people will find is one that already exists on earth ("Everyman's an angel"), which Ginsberg professes poetically elsewhere. This clash leads one to suspect that the religious symbolism in "Hymn" is formal machinery rather than authentic statement of belief, doing serious damage to the poem's integrity.

Back in Paterson after release from Rockland, Ginsberg may have shared Nikolai Berdyaev's view that "the final and infernal limit of tedium is reached when man says to himself that nothing is. Suffering is, no doubt, a relief and a salvation in such a human condition, for it is a way of regaining the depth of life. Anguish too may bring salvation. There are people who feel happy in the midst of their own and the world's emptiness, and this state may well be the supreme instance of triviality and the commonplace."[33]

The tedium Berdyaev speaks of is mirrored in the first half of Ginsberg's poem: "What do I want in these rooms papered with visions of money?" the poet asks.

How much can I make by cutting my hair? If I put new heels on my shoes,
bathe my body reeking of masturbation and sweat, layer upon layer of
    excrement
dried in employment bureaus, magazine hallways, statistical cubicles, factory
    stairways . . .

The metaphor is wages, and the age-old question of "what does it profit a man" is swept into modern idiom. "What war I enter and for what prize!" Ginsberg wearily exclaims; and the answer is readily at hand: "the dead prick of commonplace obsession, / harridan vision of electricity at night and daylight misery of thumbsucking rage" (*CP*, 40).

Not only is Berdyaev's "tedium" very much present in these lines, but also his "anguish," which "too may bring salvation." The second half of the poem presents an existential "salvation" to which Berdyaev has given the name "suffering." "Suffering" is "a way of regaining the depth of life," which Ginsberg seems instinctively to realize by defiantly choosing the beat way of life:

I would rather go mad, gone down the dark road to Mexico, heroin dripping
     in my veins,
eyes and ears full of marijuana,
eating the god Peyote on the floor of a mudhut on the border
or laying in a hotel room over the body of some suffering man or woman.

                                                                                   (*CP*, 40)

Ginsberg had done all these things—the program of anguish becomes autobiography—but for poetic purposes the catalogue of alternatives to the tedious "reality of wrath," from which he finds it imperative to escape, is engineered to inflame every moral fiber of the presumptuous "department store supervisory employee" from whom this poem is a declaration of independence. The vocabulary—the shock technique—is calculated to frighten: veins dripping with heroin, "ears full of marijuana," "the god Peyote," and illicit sex (hetero- and homosexual). The "either/or" is painted in the most vivid hues in order to verify the depth of the conviction.

Even more shocking, however, is the way Ginsberg then identifies his lurid preferences with the historical crisis of the Christian faith. It is not a shoddy attempt to usurp a respectable ally; it is a genuine declaration that his program is identical to Christ's—that he considers himself a beat Messiah. Both travel a road leading to salvation; both strive to regain the "depth of life." Says Ginsberg:

[I would] rather drag a rotten railroad tie to a Golgotha in the Rockies;
rather, crowded with thorns in Galveston, nailed hand and foot
pierced in the side in Chicago, perished and tombed in New Orleans and
     resurrected in 1958 somewhere on Garret Mountain,
come down soaring in a blaze of hot cars and garbage. . . .

                                                                                   (*CP*, 40)

Ginsberg would have liked to be a modern Christ; and, he might have thought his reconstruction of Christ's activity in the twentieth century would have had the same arresting shock value that it did two thousand years ago.

As the title page says, *Empty Mirror* is a collection of Allen Ginsberg's early poems, but it might be wise to add also the adjective "transitional." The volume gives a fairly clear picture of where Ginsberg's poetry is going, but at the same time, it is full of examples of where it has been. The technical control and concern over precise form that one sees in the front of the book are certainly indications of Ginsberg's immense debt to William Carlos Williams. As one moves further and further into *Empty Mirror*, however, one sees the Williams influence giving way to an impassioned, uninhibited style that eventually erupted as *Howl*—the subject of the next chapter.

Chapter Four
Howl and Other Poems
History of *Howl*

Despite the fact that it has been fashionable to say that *Howl* exploded on the American literary scene like a bombshell, that San Francisco finally "turned Ginsberg on," and that this poem heralded in the Beat Generation, it is difficult to find in this admittedly extraordinary poem much that has not been anticipated in inchoate and sometimes even mature form in *Empty Mirror*. *Howl* is a crystallization of incipient attitudes and techniques that Ginsberg had held for years, but it is hardly the beginning of a new poetic direction or even a sudden eruption of outrage. It cannot even be said that *Howl* is uniquely modern in form or intention. Most would have to agree with Kenneth Rexroth that this type of poetry is "in one of the oldest traditions, that of Hosea or the other angry Minor prophets of the Bible."[1] *Howl*, therefore, is not a genesis; it is an amplification.

Part of the reason for considering *Howl* an amplification has nothing to do with literature at all. The furor surrounding its initial publication was like a shot heard round the world. The poem was enshrouded by such sensationalism during the months of litigation that immediately followed its release that there was little opportunity for sober, reflective digestion of it. The press, with its appetite whetted for sensationalism rather than for impartial assessment, had a field day. Responsible commentary appeared mostly in Judge Horn's courtroom where the atmosphere was at least as much political as literary. As an example of the complete critical inadequacy with which the poem was first received, Lawrence Ferlinghetti—commenting on testimony made by a prosecution witness (an instructor from the Catholic University of San Francisco) who had remarked: "You feel like you are going through the gutter when you have to read that stuff"—observed that "the critically devastating things the prosecution's witnesses could have said but didn't, remain one of the great Catholic silences of the day."[2] If nothing else, the legal proceedings brought against *Howl* for obscenity served to make it easily one of the best-selling volumes of poetry of the twentieth century.

Howl was published by Ferlinghetti's City Lights Books in San Francisco as a part of the Pocket Poets Series. The first edition was printed in England by Villiers, passed through United States Customs, and was subsequently delivered to San Francisco for publication in the fall of 1956. A series of almost comical legal interventions then led to the "obscenity" trial, which eventually pronounced *Howl and Other Poems* as *not* being without "the slightest redeeming social importance." In other words, in the eyes of the court, it was found not to be obscene.

The first event leading to the trial occurred on 24 March 1957, when a portion of a second printing of the volume was stopped by custom officials on the basis of section 305 of the Tariff Act of 1930. The *San Francisco Chronicle* quoted Chester MacPhee, the collector of customs, as saying that "the words and the sense of the writing is obscene. You wouldn't want your children to come across it."[3] Shortly afterward, the American Civil Liberties Union objected to the action after having read the manuscript supplied to it by the publisher Ferlinghetti. While this litigation was going on, a new edition of *Howl* was being printed in the United States, which took it out of the jurisdiction of customs.

A little over a month later, Ferlinghetti published an article in the *San Francisco Chronicle* in which, as he himself paraphrases, "I recommend a medal be made for Collector MacPhee, since his action was already rendering the book famous. But the police were soon to take over this advertising account and do a much better job—10,000 copies of *Howl* were in print by the time they finished with it." In a more serious vein, Ferlinghetti went on to say, "It is not the poet but what he observes which is revealed as obscene. The great obscene wastes of *Howl* are the sad wastes of the mechanized world, lost among atom bombs and insane nationalisms."[4]

The stand of the customs officials crumbled shortly afterward when the United States attorney in San Francisco refused to act against *Howl*; the books were released. But this was only an interlude. Within a week, Ferlinghetti was arrested by a representative of the juvenile department ("Well named, in this case," Ferlinghetti wryly remarked) of the San Francisco Police Department.[5] The American Civil Liberties Union posted bail, but the fight had started.

Ferlinghetti documented a representative selection of critical support for *Howl* in his article "Horn on *Howl*," published in the *Evergreen Review*. A few random excerpts provide some appreciation of a rare situation in which a literary production received unqualified praise. "I only wish to say that the book is a thoroughly serious work of literary art" (Henry Rago, editor of *Poetry*); "*Howl and Other Poems* . . . is a dignified, sincere and admirable work of art" (William Hogan, *San Francisco Chronicle*); "The poet gives us the most painful details; he moves toward a statement of experience that is challenging and finally noble" (Robert Duncan and Ruth Witt-Diamant, San Francisco poets); "*Howl* is one of the most important books of poetry published in the last ten years" (Thomas Parkinson, University of California); "the book has considerable distinction as literature, being a powerful and artistic expression of a meaningful philosophical attitude" (James Laughlin, New Directions publisher).[6]

In the course of the trial, numerous witnesses for the defense offered more detailed explication of the poet's intent—but with no less lavish praise. Most informative are the testimonies of professor Mark Schorer of the University of California and Kenneth Rexroth. The following portion of Schorer's testimony from the trial transcript was reprinted in Ferlinghetti's *Evergreen Review* article:

The theme of the poem is announced very clearly in the opening line. . . . Then the following lines that make up the first part attempt to create the impression of a kind of nightmare world in which people representing "the best minds of my generation," in the author's view, are wandering like damned souls in hell. That is done through a kind of series of what one might call surrealistic images, a kind of state of hallucinations. Then in the second section the mood of the poem changes and it becomes an indictment of those elements in modern society that, in the author's view, are destructive of the best qualities in human nature and of the best minds. Those elements are, I would say, predominantly materialism, conformity and mechanization leading toward war. And then the third part is a personal address to a friend, real or fictional, of the poet or of the person who is speaking in the poet's voice—those are not always the same thing—who is mad and in a madhouse, and is the specific representative of what the author regards as a general condition.(151–52)

Schorer provides as good a statement of the structure, theme, and general strategy of the poem as is possible under the circumstances. In his testimony Kenneth Rexroth associates *Howl* with biblical tradition, evincing sophisticated forensic tactics as well as an acute literary perspicuity:

The simplest term for such writing is prophetic, it is easier to call it that than anything else because we have a large body of prophetic writing to refer to. There are the prophets of the Bible, which [*Howl*] greatly resembles in purpose and in language and in subject matter. . . . The theme is the denunciation of evil and a pointing out of the way out, so to speak. That is prophetic literature. "Woe! Woe! Woe! The City of Jerusalem! The Syrian is about to come down or has already and you are to do such and such a thing and you must repent and do thus and so." And *Howl*, the four parts of the poem—that is including the "Footnote to *Howl*," of course, again, is Biblical in reference. The reference is to the Benedicite, which says over and over again, "Blessed is the fire, Blessed is the light, Blessed are the trees, and Blessed is this and Blessed is that," and [Ginsberg] is saying "Everything that is human is Holy to me," and that the possibility of salvation in his terrible situation which he reveals is through love and through the love of everything Holy in man. So that, I would say, that this just about covers the field of typically prophetic poetry. (154)

This early criticism points out the two decisive and negative poles in most of Ginsberg's subsequent poetry: existential despair and the implicit optimism of scriptural prophecy. Since the issue of the trial was quickly pared down to the question of *Howl*'s social relevance, aesthetic considerations were held in abeyance.

The Poem

In *Howl*, Ginsberg explains in 1969, "what I was digging . . . was the *humor* of exhibitionism. You're free to say any damn thing you want; but people are so scared of hearing you say what's unconsciously universal that it's comical. So I wrote with an element of comedy— partly intended to soften the blow."[7] *Howl* was from the first taken so seriously as a political, social, and literary cause célèbre that its comic quality has been generally ignored by critics and social historians. Not by the poet himself, however. William A. Henry III describing Ginsberg's reading of *Howl* at the McMillin Theater at Columbia in 1981 is stunned that "this puckish little figure, this professorial imp with the loony grin, does not sound angry. He is not wailing about the wickedness of his time. . . . The audience is laughing with him. They are howling, but in pleasure rather than anger, as he thrusts an arm up for each of the jokes. They hear satire, not nobly expended pain."[8] Henry senses that "something has changed" since Ginsberg's first reading of *Howl* at Six Gallery in San Francisco a quarter century earlier—that the older poet "is mocking the past—

mocking the angry radicals, mocking the dreamers, mocking the quest for visions." Maybe so. Ginsberg and American society have both changed. But we should not let this deceive us to think that the comic mockery in *Howl* is simply a recent, accidental accretion; it was inherent in *Howl* from the beginning.

Howl was "typed out madly in one afternoon," Ginsberg tells us, "a tragic custard-pie comedy of wild phrasing, meaningless images for the beauty of abstract poetry of mind running along making awkward combinations like Charley Chaplin's walk, long saxophone-like chorus lines I knew Kerouac would hear *sound* of—Taking off from his own inspired prose line really a new poetry."[9] The words Ginsberg uses to describe his state—*madly, custard-pie comedy, wild, meaningless, Charley Chaplin*—all speak to a sense of creative freedom, the aggressive irresponsibility of unrestrained whimsy and the deliberate indifference to personal and literary inhibitions of any sort. It was, as Ginsberg says, an act of comic exhibitionism effected through a deliberate exorcism of fear. "I thought I wouldn't write a *poem*," he explains, "but just write what I wanted to without fear, let my imagination go, open secrecy, and scribble magic lines from my real mind—sum up my life—something I wouldn't be able to show anybody, write for my own soul's ear and a few other golden ears." Ginsberg sought a liberation from the inhibitions of shame; "Shame," he once said, "is just one aspect of fear."[10]

But *Howl* was also a declaration of metrical freedom. While in retrospect Ginsberg often accommodates the literati by attempting to classify his metrical form ("like [in] certain passages of *Howl* and certain passages of *Kaddish*—there are definite rhythms which could be analyzed as corresponding to classical rhythms, though not necessarily *English* classical rhythms, or Sanskrit prosody," at the moment of creation he insists that he is "working with my own neural impulses and writing impulses."[11] He then explains the technique in a way that suggests the full extent of the sort of metrical freedom *Howl* demonstrates:

> I wasn't really working with a classical unit, I
> was working with my own neural impulses and writing
> impulses. See, the difference is between someone
> sitting down to write a poem *in* a definite preconceived
> metrical pattern and filling in that pattern, and
> someone working with physiological movements and

> arriving at a pattern, and perhaps even arriving at a
> pattern which might even have a name, or might even
> have a classical usage, but arriving at it organically
> rather than synthetically. Nobody's got any objection
> to even iambic pentameter if it comes from a source
> deeper than the mind, that is to say if it comes from
> the breathing and the belly and the lungs.[12]

The first part of *Howl* is a list of the atrocities that have allegedly
been endured by Ginsberg and his friends. More generally, these
atrocities accumulate to form a desperate critique of a civilization that
has set up a power structure that determines people's "mode of consciousness . . . sexual enjoyments . . . different labors and . . .
loves."[13] The theme is clearly the same as Ginsberg's essay "Poetry,
Violence, and the Trembling Lambs" in which he pleads: "When will
we discover an America that will not deny its own God Who takes
up arms, money, police, and a million hands to murder the consciousness of God Who spits in the beautiful face of Poetry which
sings the Glory of God and weeps in the dust of the world?"[14]

This is prose, but it could easily be inserted into the text of *Howl*
without change. Even the structural device of the recurring word *who*
is exploited, which demonstrates how blurred, even nonexistent, is
the line between poetry and prose in Ginsberg's work. The word *who*,
Ginsberg has explained, was used in *Howl* "to keep the beat, a base
to keep measure, return to and take off from again onto another streak
of invention."[15] One might even say that *who* was Ginsberg's point of
contact between vision and reality—an anchor that regularly brought
his free flights back to earth and kept the poem from disappearing
into the mists of a subjective wasteland.

Who, it can be said, also served as an organizational excuse; by its
sanction, otherwise unrelated chunks of inspiration could be thrown
spontaneously into the poem. In other words, the device was a structural shield that kept "thinking" at bay, thereby allowing imaginative illumination and association unlimited freedom. Ginsberg's
reiterative device suggests, of course, the influence of Whitman. As
Gay Wilson Allen points out, "Whitman's parallelism, or thought
rhythm, is so often accompanied and reinforced by parallel wording
and sounds that the two techniques are often almost identical. An
easy way to collect examples of Whitman's 'thought rhythm' is to
glance down the left-hand margin and notice the lines beginning with

the same word, and usually the same grammatical construction: 'I will . . . I will . . . I will . . .' or 'Where . . . Where . . . Where . . .' or 'When . . . When . . . When. . . .' etc."[16]

Such a technique is indicative of a poetic movement that is cumulative rather than logical or progressive, as Allen also observes; and it is uniquely suited to what he calls an "expanding ego psychology." Such a psychology, to follow Allen's argument further, "results in an enumerative style, the cataloging of a representative and symbolical succession of images, conveying the sensation of pantheistic unity and endless becoming." Ginsberg's supreme celebration of "pantheistic unity" is nowhere better sought than in "Footnote to *Howl*." The cumulative technique also goes back to the Hebraic roots that Ginsberg acknowledges as influences upon his work; and Allen notes that "the Hebraic poet developed a rhythm of thought, repeating and balancing ideas and sentences (or independent clauses) instead of syllables or accents."[17]

This criticism of Whitman is relative to *Howl* not only because Ginsberg's poetry exploits the devices of accumulation and parallelism but also because the unit of the poem is so decisively the line, even when the particular line is attenuated to meet the demands of an inspirational flight. E. C. Ross's point about the line in Whitman's poetry could also be applied to Ginsberg's *Howl*. "Whitman's verse," says Ross, "with the exception that it is not metered—is farther removed from prose than is traditional verse itself, for the reason that the traditional verse is, like prose, composed in sentences, whereas Whitman's verse is composed in lines. . . . A run-on line is rare in Whitman. . . . The law of his structure is that *the unit of sense is the measure of the line*."[18] Precisely the same law of structure holds true for Ginsberg's *Howl* showing the extent of his debt to Whitman, as well as providing a rationale for regarding *Howl* as poetry.

To read *Howl* properly, then, is to avoid the impulse to search for a logic or a rational connection of ideas, as Ginsberg would be the first to acknowledge. *Howl* must be read the same way as Whitman's poetry, but with a twentieth-century consciousness. Ginsberg himself has lamented that "everybody assumes . . . that [Whitman's] line is a big freakish uncontrollable necessary prosaic goof. No attempt's been made to use it in the light of early XX Century organization of new speech-rhythm prosody to *build up* large organic structures."[19] *Howl* seems to be an experiment along these lines.

The yardsticks to measure the worth of the first part of *Howl* are basically two: the "tightness" of the catalogue and the maintenance of spontaneity. The first measurement has to do with what Ginsberg calls "density"—the richness of imagery packed into a given line. By and large, the poem does achieve density. Some might object that such richness is achieved at the cost of grammatical coherence. The same objection could be leveled at Whitman's verse, and further, since the movement of the poem is not logical but cumulative, grammar not only ceases to become a serious concern, but may very well be an impediment to one's contact with reality. "Nature herself has no grammar," says Ernest Fenollosa, and so the classical grammarians' definition of the sentence as "a complete thought" or as a construction "uniting subject and predicate" is simply at odds with reality. There is no completeness in nature and therefore there should be no completeness in the sentence. "The sentence . . . is not an attribute of Nature but an accident of man as a conversational animal."[20] It is no accident that the entire seventy-eight-line first section counts grammatically as a single sentence.

A substantial portion of the poem's density is also supplied by the method Ginsberg derived from Cézanne's optic tricks—the *petites sensations*. Their verbal equivalents in *Howl* are such juxtapositions as "negro streets," "angry fix," "paint hotels," "blind streets," "Peyote solidities," "hydrogen jukebox," and so on endlessly throughout the poem. "I used a lot of [Cézanne's] material in the references in the last part of the first section of *Howl*: 'sensation of Pater Omnipotens Aeterna Deus,'" Ginsberg has said. "The last part of *Howl* was really an homage to Cézanne's method, in a sense I adapted what I could to writing."[21]

The second measuring stick for evaluating *Howl* is its spontaneity. "But how sustain a long line in poetry (lest it lapse into prosaic)?" Ginsberg asked himself.[22] One potent answer is Olson's "projective" principle: "ONE PERCEPTION MUST IMMEDIATELY AND DIRECTLY LEAD TO A FURTHER PERCEPTION." If this dogma can be summarized in a word, it is *speed*. Spontaneity lives on speed, and the creating poet must avoid the lag. He does so, it seems, through association. There are many examples operative in the first part of *Howl*, but Ginsberg has specifically described the principle with reference to part two. He begins with a feeling, he says, that develops into something like a sigh. Then he looks around for the object that is making him sigh; then he "sigh[s] in words." At best, he goes on, he finds a word or several words that become key to the feeling, and he builds on

them to complete the statement. "It's simply by a process of association that I find what the rest of the statement is, what can be collected around that word, what that word is connected to." He then
demonstrates the process specifically:

Partly by simple association, the first thing that comes to my mind like
"Moloch is" or "Moloch who," and then whatever comes out. But that also
goes along with a definite rhythmic impulse, like DA de de DA de de DA
de de DA DA. "*Mo*loch whose *eyes* are a *thous*and blind *windows.*" And before
I wrote "Moloch whose eyes are a thousand blind windows," I had the word,
"Moloch, Moloch, Moloch," and I also had the feeling DA de de DA de de
DA de de DA DA. So it was just a question of looking up and seeing a lot
of windows, and saying, oh, windows, of course, but what kind of windows?
But not even that—"Moloch whose eyes." "Moloch whose *eyes*"—which is
beautiful in itself—but what about it, Moloch whose eyes are *what?* "Thou-
sands blind." And I had to finish it somehow. So I hadda say "windows." It
looked good *afterward.*[23]

Ginsberg emphasizes the word *afterward* because the spontaneity of
his poetry depends upon the existentialist formula: existence precedes
essence. While he is writing, he is living (existing) through the experience. Thought about that experience (essence) would reduce the immediacy of the experience itself—even make it secondhand—and so,
as Ginsberg says, "usually during the composition, step by step,
word by word and adjective by adjective, if it's at all spontaneous, I
don't know whether it even makes sense sometimes."[24] Spontaneity
seems to require suspension of the rational faculties for the purpose of
permitting the logic of the heart to operate freely. Testimony for this
assertion is Ginsberg's own: "Sometimes I do know it makes complete
sense, and I start crying."[25] Clearly, *Howl,* like most of Ginsberg's
work, follows a grammar of emotion. The "verification principle" is
shifted from the logical positivists' tests—Can I see it, smell it, taste
it, hear it, or feel it?—to the simplest test of the heart: "Does it
make me cry?"

Any analysis or explication of *Howl* would seem an affront to the
poem's very method, which is literally a violent howl of spontaneous,
suprarational feeling. Ex post facto explanation appears an almost certain way of completely missing the point. Nevertheless, a few gener-
alizations and observations may prove helpful guideposts through this
"animal cry" of human anguish. First, the poet sets himself up as ob-
server in the opening line. He is witness to the destruction of "the

best minds of my generation" by madness (*CP*, 126). "Madness presumably is the state of civilization that the poet understands as hostile to the sentient martyrs whose collective experiences under its tyranny are catalogued in a cumulative, cresting wave of relative clauses. Second, at the same time, madness occurs thematically in the first part of the poem in other forms. For example, it is suggested that these martyrs have been attracted to what is implied as a mad quest: they are "burning for the ancient heavenly connection to the starry dynamo in the machinery of the night," and they have "bared their brains to Heaven" (*CP*, 126). Farther along in the poem it is mentioned that they "thought they were *only* mad when Baltimore gleamed in supernatural ecstasy [italics added]" (*CP*, 127), which is later followed by a reference to Ginsberg's own commitment to an asylum (*CP*, 130), and finally the specific application of the madness theme to a specific individual, Carl Solomon, who is undergoing treatment at Rockland State Hospital (*CP*, 130).

There is a degree of ambivalence in the use of this crucial term *madness* in the first line. Does it reflect merely the "madness" of an officially acceptable level of reality that is uncongenial to the suffering heroes of the poem, or is it not possible that this destructive "madness" also describes the predicament of nonconformists? In other words, are not these martyrs self-destroyed because they refuse to live on the acceptable plane of official reality? In these terms, the "angel-headed hipsters" are embracing "madness" as an alternative to an unbearable sanity. Their madness consists in their refusal to accept a nonspiritual view of the world, in their "burning for the ancient heavenly connection" in a civilization that has proclaimed that God is dead. For this reason, Ginsberg emphasizes their thinking "they were only mad when Baltimore gleamed in supernatural ecstasy" (*CP*, 127).[26]

Nevertheless, a tension is created in the poem between planes of reality that are differentiated in terms of time. The "hipsters" undergo a pilgrimage through "blind streets of shuddering cloud and lightning of the mind" (*CP*, 126), which illuminates "all the motionless world of Time, between / Peyote solidities of halls . . ." (*CP*, 126), and so on. This time is supernatural, eternal—not the chronological time of unilluminated existence. Peyote is a chemical channel to timelessness, and the "lightening of the mind" is a *petite sensation* that is a gap in time itself. Among other things, the "hipster" pilgrimage is a journey out of time and the insufferable plane of reality it represents. Because of this journey, the pilgrims "threw their watches off the roof to cast their ballot for Eternity outside of Time, & alarm clocks fell on their heads every day for the next decade" (*CP*, 129). For pursuing "timelessness," the "hipsters" are punished by "Time"; and the symbol of the tyrannical alarm clocks is particularly effective because of their association with the humdrum, inhuman requirements of the "square world."

Christian parallels are unavoidable. The persecution of the early followers of Christ in Roman catacombs finds its counterpart in the despair of those "who lit cigarettes in boxcars boxcars boxcars racketing through snow toward lonesome farms in the grandfather night" (*CP*, 127), and those "who were burned alive in their innocent flannel suits in Madison Avenue amid blasts of leaden verse . . . or were run down by the drunken taxicabs of Absolute Reality" (*CP*, 129). Finally, there is Carl Solomon, the supreme martyr—the archetype who is "really in the total animal soup of time" (*CP*, 130)—to whom the poem is addressed.

Part two of *Howl*, written under the influence of peyote, is an accusation: "What sphinx of cement and aluminum bashed open their skulls and ate up their brains and imagination?" (*CP*, 131). The protagonist "who" is now replaced, in an attempt to coordinate the structures of the two sections, by the antagonist "Moloch." The spontaneity of this part is vitiated not so much because Ginsberg violates the principles of rapid associations and the like, but because the element of surprise is gone. The unraveling of the *j'accuse* is painfully inevitable, and Ginsberg is thrown back upon the single resource of imagery. The effect of the *petites sensation* has by this time been blunted almost to the point of tedium, and the voice of the propagandist begins to usurp that of the poet. The case is almost identical with the much criticized Usury canto of Ezra Pound. Without the sauce of the unexpected, Ginsberg's Hebraic lamentations on Moloch become increasingly difficult to digest as they drag on to the conclusion where the "Mad generation" is hurled "down on the rocks of Time" (*CP*, 132).

Part three begins suspiciously like a "peptalk" or a get-well card: "Carl Solomon! I'm with you in Rockland where you're madder than I am" (*CP*, 132). Whether this assertion is diagnosis or flattery hinges on the connotation one chooses for madness. Solomon, however, has been raised, through the bulk of accumulation, to the status of a symbol. The final section of the poem unfolds as a dark version of Donne's "Seventeenth Meditation." Certainly, "no man is an island," but Donne never could have anticipated such lines as "I'm with you in Rockland where we hug and kiss the United States under our bedsheets," or "I'm with you in Rockland where you accuse your doctors of insanity and plot the Hebrew socialist revolution against the fascist national Golgotha" (*CP*, 133).

Whether the following explanation Ginsberg gave for the total pattern of *Howl* was premeditation or afterthought, even he would probably decline to say; but it does supply a workable rationale for the project: "Part I, a lament for the Lamb in America with instances of remarkable lamblike youths; Part II names the monster of mental consciousness that preys on the Lamb; Part III a litany of affirmation of the Lamb in its glory: 'O starry-spangled shock of Mercy!' The structure of Part II, pyramidal, with a graduated longer response to the fixed base."[27]

Ginsberg considers "Footnote to *Howl*" as the last of a series of experiments with a fixed base. "I set it as Footnote to *Howl* because it was an extra variation of the form of Part II,"[28] he explains. "Moloch," the symbols of social illness, was the metrical anchor in part two for a series of graphic but predictable images. Since "Footnote" presumes to offer a cure for the social illness (Moloch), it is appropriate that the structure of both sections be roughly parallel and that the word *Holy* should operate in the same manner as its counterpart, *Moloch*. In this way a symmetrical balance is achieved both structurally and thematically. A simple comparison of a line from each section picked at random immediately shows Ginsberg's conscious exploitation of structural balance for thematic purposes:

> Moloch whose eyes are a thousand blind windows! Moloch whose
> skyscrapers stand in the long streets like endless Jehovahs!
> Moloch whose factories dream and croak in the fog!
> Moloch whose smokestacks and antennae crown the cities!
> (*CP*, 131)

. . . .

> Holy the solitudes of skyscrapers and pavements! Holy the
> cafeterias filled with millions! Holy the mysterious
> rivers of tears under the streets!
> (*CP*, 134)

Clearly, the distinction between "Moloch" and "Holy" is point of view. One is confronted with identical raw material in both cases (skyscrapers, pavements, and urban commonplaces), but the subjective perspective yields two separate appraisals. On the one hand, there is ugliness; on the other, an understanding of the holiness of everything. The response depends upon how one looks at the world.

If Moloch is a state of mind that is the dark side of a holy state of mind, how does one differentiate between the two attitudes with any precision? Ginsberg once again appears to resort to time as his touchstone. Part two ends in a rhetorical fury that describes, among a plethora of other things, a "Mad generation! down on the rocks of Time!" (*CP*, 132). Similarly, "Footnote" contains near its conclusion the somewhat enigmatic line:

> Holy time in eternity holy eternity in time holy the
> clocks in space holy the fourth dimension holy the
> fifth International holy the Angel in Moloch!

Two distinct understandings of time are exhibited in these lines: on the one hand, there is a destructive time, which belongs to the realm of Moloch and which scuttles the "mad generation" upon its craggy surface; on the other hand, there is the paradoxical time of holiness, where time and eternity (logical opposites) are reconciled presumably in the "fourth dimension." To simplify an excessively complicated idea, it appears that Ginsberg is merely attempting to differentiate between an objective, chronological timekeeping, with its attendant implications of responsibility, duty, and competition, and a subjective, Bergsonian temporal measurement that understands time only as it is relative to human existence. Time, therefore, becomes a symbol of two separate realms of existence: "squares" read time on their wristwatches; "hipsters" read the holy "clocks in space," which inform that time does not matter—that the truth is timeless.

The concern for objective time, then, is not merely a symptom of Moloch's activity in the world; it is the very activity itself. Time is the natural enemy of holiness because holiness is discovered through love. One need go no further than traditional love poetry to be convinced that time is the natural opponent of love, but Ginsberg presumes to carry this natural antagonism to its extreme by implying that the modern obsession with objective time prevents one from experiencing a true community with others. The enigmatic assertion in "Footnote"—"Who digs Los Angeles IS Los Angeles" (*CP*, 134)—serves to sum up, in a way, Ginsberg's whole attitude towards time.

Time to him is always present tense because he acknowledges only time which is "lived through." Los Angeles, for example, is not just a place existing at a certain time; Los Angeles is a human being's concerned impression of Los Angeles. For that concerned person, Los Angeles exists only when he or she is "digging" it. In that sense, the individual is a solipsist of sorts who creates the reality of Los Angeles in the mind, timeless and placeless, holy and eternal.

Other Poems

Appearing with the notorious *Howl* in the 1956 volume are several other poems of significance. One of the best, "In the Baggage Room at Greyhound," is a vividly rendered, four-part meditation that effectively transforms the detailed reality of a bus station baggage room into a metaphysical allegory:

it was the racks and these on the racks I saw naked in electric light the night
    before I quit,
the racks were created to hang our possessions, to keep us together, a
    temporary shift in space,
God's only way of building the rickety structure of Time,
to hold the bags to send on the roads, to carry our luggage from place to
    place
looking for a bus to ride us back home to Eternity where the heart was left
    and farewell tears began.

                                                              (*CP*, 154)

It is not the allegory nor the symbolism that makes this poem work so well; it is, as so consistently is the case, Ginsberg's eye. In line with meditative tradition to which it belongs, "In the Baggage Room at Greyhound" scrutinizes the smallest physical objects in order to "find Heaven in a grain of sand."

"Sunflower Sutra" (*CP*, 138) is somewhat anticipated by the earlier "In back of the real" (*CP*, 113). The themes of both are essentially the same, but "In back of the real" exhibits Ginsberg's early flirtation with Williams's short-line method, while "Sunflower Sutra" demonstrates his advance toward the "Melvillian bardic breath" long-line technique. Both poems present flowers seen against backdrops of a railroad yard in San Jose and a "tincan banana dock," respectively. In "In back of the real," the flower is a symbolic martyr ("It had a / brittle black stem and corolla of yellowish dirty / spikes like Jesus' inchlong crown. . . .") that suffers under the oppressive grime of industrialization. It is a "flower of industry, tough spikey ugly flower." Both Jesus and the flower are understood as bearing the sins of humanity, the adjective "spikey" even suggesting a vague allusion to the stigmata. The point of the poem, which the title explicitly proclaims, is that, despite the ugliness of the exterior of the flower, it is a "flower nonetheless, with the form of the great yellow Rose of your brain / This is the flower of the World."

The word *real* in the title is meant to represent only the external appearance of the inherent, natural reality of "flowerness," which remains constant underneath the filth of civilization. In *back* of the real (the ugliness) the poet finds an almost platonic formal reality, and the situation of the flower is seen to be an emblem of the present human situation. In short, the theme is hardly different from the theme of "Footnote to *Howl*" where it is proclaimed that "Everything is holy" in its root nature and is discoverable through love.

The similar themes of the earlier and the later poems permit one to appreciate some of the radical effects that are achieved with the introduction of the long line. The later poem, "Sunflower Sutra," is a complete metamorphosis and a far more genuine article. Why? The first poem is spare, economical, and contains the striking comparison of the flower with Christ. Although it is written in the first person, the general tone is rather formal. The focus of attention is upon the flower, not upon the perceiver of the flower. In short, the poem has the rudiments of a classical quality to it—classical at least as Williams would use the term. The short line has produced a control that saturates the structure of the poem, even permeating to the treatment of what is intended as a highly personal epiphany.

Contrast this feeling of control with the mood in "Sunflower Sutra," and the tremendous difference between a relatively good early poem and a later one can be seen in an instant. The distinction totally transcends structure, but structure is its genesis. The intimacy of the first person, to begin with, is expanded through the introduction of a second persona—Jack Kerouac. The description of the scene (structurally a sine qua non in both poems) is developed much more expansively, because of the meditative possibilities of the long line. Dramatic narrative enters the poem, increasing the immediacy and personal intimacy of the moment, so that, when the flower is discovered ("Look at the Sunflower, he said . . . I rushed up enchanted . . . ."), a kinetic energy is released that begins a buildup of emotion impossible in the earlier poem. Finally, there is no hint of artifice in "Sunflower Sutra." It is completely natural and completely in the present. There is no scavenging of the past for significant allusion; the immediate ingredients of what is under the nose accomplish everything without assistance, save for the concluding sermon, and make explicit what was implicit in "In back of the real."

The transition from the short-line form to the long, with its attendant changes in tone, charts the course of Ginsberg's poetry from what might be termed conventional, literary verse to Kerouac's ideal of "spontaneous prose." As Ginsberg has said, "Of course the distinctions between prose and poetry are broken down anyway. So much that I was saying like a long page of oceanic Kerouac is sometimes as sublime as epic line."[29] What Ginsberg finds so attractive in the long line is, therefore, its possibilities for honestly and without deception telling the truth (which for Ginsberg is, at this stage in his life, inward). The formal devices of traditional poetry are for him hypocritical. For these reasons Ginsberg was so astounded, as he reports it, when Kerouac told him one night "that in the future literature would consist of what people actually wrote rather than what they tried to deceive other people into thinking they wrote, when they revised it later on."[30]

"America" (*CP*, 146)—about as spontaneous as a poem can be—is whimsical, sad, comic, tedious, honest, bitter, impatient, and yet, somehow, incisive. It refuses to settle on a consistent structure. Dialogue discovers that it is monologue and then drifts off into mutterings against a hypothetical national alter ego. The poem is an attempt to catch the mood of a particular attitude toward the United States without the interference of logic. It is a drunken poet arguing after hours with a drunken nation; and yet, through all the turmoil, the gibberish, and the illogicality, a broad-based attack, which rational discourse can only hint at, is launched against American values. The seemingly hopeless illogicality of the poem itself becomes a mirror for the hopeless illogicality it reflects.

Interspersed throughout the poem are lines that suggest almost all the attitudes, postures, and convictions of Ginsberg's earlier poems. First and foremost is the souring of Whitman's exuberant optimism toward America into a disillusionment that suggests the breaking of a covenant: "America I've given you all and now I'm nothing" (*CP*, 146). This admission is followed later in the poem by an appeal to America to shake off its hypocrisy and be equal to Whitman's chal-

lenge: "America when will you be angelic? / When will you take off
your clothes?" (*CP*, 146). The motif of "one time / is all Time if you
look / at it out of the grave" earlier articulated in "In Death, Cannot
Reach What Is Most Near" (*CP*, 34), comes directly afterward
("When will you look at yourself through the grave?"), shortly followed by the here-and-now position previously taken in "Metaphysics" (*CP*, 33): "America after all it is you and I who are perfect not
the next world" (*CP*, 146).

The characteristic Zen antagonism toward striving and competition
is also represented significantly in "America":

> I'm obsessed by Time Magazine . . .
> It's always telling me about responsibility. Business men
>   are serious
>   Movie producers are serious. Everybody's serious but
>   me.
>
>   (*CP*, 147)

And so the poem continues in a jerky dialogue full of shifting issues,
which only at the conclusion bothers to justify its nonsensical logic
and its logical nonsense: "America this is the impression I get from
looking in the television set. / America is this correct?" (*CP*, 148).

The real impact of the protest in this poem is conveyed structurally. The scattered irritations and objections are merely instrumental
caprice; it is the total bewilderment and confusion that one feels in
reading the poem rather than the validity of the attacks that quicken
one's appreciation of the American dilemma Ginsberg attempts to
mirror.

"A Supermarket in California" (*CP*, 136) is another study of the
contrasts between Whitman's America and Ginsberg's. True to the
American idiom, the poet is pictured as "shopping for images" in
the "supermarket" of American life, dreaming all the while of Whitman's "enumerations." Here is poet as consumer filling his shopping
cart for the ingredients of his art among "Aisles full of husbands!"
Implicit in his meditations is the question: What would Whitman
have thought of America now? A dramatic reconstruction takes place:
"I saw you, Walt Whitman, childless, lonely old grubber, / poking
among the meats in the refrigerator and eyeing the grocery boys."

The poet follows Whitman "in and out of the brilliant stacks of
cans" (follows him also, in fact, in poetic technique), imaginatively

feeling the presence of the "store detective" behind them. Even here, Ginsberg cannot help underscoring the illicitness of the poet's position in society—both his own and Whitman's. No doubt Ginsberg's many brushes with the authorities helped nourish his obsession that the way of the true poet inevitably arouses police suspicion. But the poet can always enjoy freedom of the mind, which is suggested in the following lines:

> We strode down the open corridors together in our
> solitary fancy tasting artichokes, possessing every frozen
> delicacy, and never passing the cashier.
>
> (*CP*, 136)

Fortunately, images cost nothing; they have already been paid for by those who have put them up for display, and this fact leads to the final meditation of the last stanza.

"Where are we going, Walt Whitman? The doors close in an hour. Which way does your beard point tonight?" Ginsberg asks. The urgency of the *quo vadis* adds pathos to the appeal. There is not much time. What are the options, old "graybeard"? Will they continue their alien course? "Will we walk all night through solitary streets? . . . we'll both be lonely." Or will the poet and Whitman give up on their country and "stroll dreaming of the lost America of love past blue automobiles in driveways, home to our silent cottage"? Despair and nostalgia seem the two alternatives, and the disciple is bewildered.

The poem ends, as it inevitably must, with a question:

> Ah, dear father, graybeard, lonely old courage-teacher.
> What America did you have when Charon quit poling his ferry
> and you got out on a smoking bank and stood watching the
> boat disappear on the black waters of Lethe?
>
> (*CP*, 136)

Whitman's America was quite different from the one Ginsberg sees around him, and the next poem in the collection, "Transcripts of Organ Music," follows Ginsberg "home to our silent cottage" where he ponders his existential misery to a Zen beat.

The poem is quite simply the description of a moment—a timeless moment when an event occurs. The event is nothing more sensational than "a moment of clarity" when the poet "saw the feeling in the heart of things [and] walked out into the garden crying." The moment sounds very similar to one of Wordsworth's "time spots" or mystic visions, but the reference in Ginsberg's poem is decidedly oriental. The mood is what in Zen would be called *wabi*, an instance, in Alan Watts's words, "when the artist is feeling depressed or sad, and in this particular emptiness of feeling catches a glimpse of something rather ordinary and unpretentious in its incredible 'suchness.' "[31]

The opening two-line stanza roughly approximates two haiku poems and serves as a kind of introduction, or perhaps frame, for the body proper of the work:

The flower in the glass peanut bottle formerly in the kitchen crooked to take
    a place in the light,
the closet door opened, because I used it before, it kindly stayed open
    waiting for me, its owner.

                                                                (*CP*, 140)

Then comes the articulation of the *wabi*: "I began to feel my misery in pallet on floor, listening to music, my misery, that's why I want to sing."

Two concepts are of paramount importance to understanding the movement of this poem. One is the expectation of "the presence of the Creator" (*satori*), and the other is the attempt to dissolve all conflict between man and nature. The medium in which both phenomena occur is timelessness—the absence of hurry, rush, urgency, when "the human senses are fully open to receive the world" (Watts, 171). The beginning of the "moment of clarity" occurs when the poet, listening to the music, realizes that his "gray painted walls and ceiling" contained him "as the sky contained . . . [his] garden." An equation is grasped between himself and nature; it is understood particularly in flowers.

In attempting to transcribe the affinity, even the oneness, between himself and flowers,[32] he runs into the Zen problem of creation; for, according to the principles of Zen, to expend effort in creation is to lose precisely the ability to create. As the poem puts it, "Can I bring back the words? Will thought of transcription haze my mental open eye?" (*CP*, 140). Thinking is not the answer to transcription here, for "the Taoist mentally makes, or forces, nothing but 'grows' everything" (Watts, 171). Hence, Ginsberg's next line becomes clear: "the kindly search for growth, the gracious desire to exist of / the flowers, my near ecstasy at existing among them. . . ." The problem, then, is not to write about a flower or an experience of a flower, but to become a flower. Zen masters, supervising the art training of their pupils, watch them as "a gardener watches the growth of a tree, and wants to have his student to have the attitude of the tree" (Watts, 171).

Time and the responsibilities that time imply are foreign to this moment, and so books on the table are described as "waiting in space where I placed them, they haven't disappeared, time's left its remains and qualities for me to use" (*CP*, 140). This is a moment, in other words, expanded, but not endless. Time has literally stopped in order that an "openness" to things can occur. As Watts observes, "It is only when there is no goal and no rush that the human senses are fully open to receive the world" (171), and this is precisely what happens during the "glimpse of clarity" in the poem. It is a celebration of "openness" to the world, which is structurally held together by the initial and subsequent references to the open closet door. "I looked up," the poet says, "those red bush blossoms . . . their leaves . . . upturned top flat to the sky to receive—all creation open to receive . . ." (*CP*, 140–41).

There are other "openings" as well—a catalogue of them. There is a light socket open "to receive a plug which . . . serves my phonograph now . . ."; the doorless entry to the kitchen; "the door to the womb was open to admit me if I wished to enter"; the "unused electricity plugs all over my house if I ever need them"; the open kitchen window. Significantly, only the potential openness of the telephone is nonfunctional at this moment; the telephone is an openness to time that is for the present suspended. This enumeration of "connections" Ginsberg provides for his own consideration—connections that bind together humans and nature, nature and the cosmos. It is Ginsberg's way of expressing the Zen insight that "if we open our eyes and see clearly, it becomes obvious that there is no other time than this instant, and that the past and the future are abstractions without any concrete reality" (Watts, 192). The poet Hung Tzu-ch'eng puts it thus: "If the mind is not overlaid with wind and waves, you will always be living among blue mountains and green trees. If your true nature has the creative force of Nature itself, wherever you may go, you will see fishes leaping and geese flying."[33]

Chapter Five
Kaddish

Allen Ginsberg regularly insists that "everything I write is in one way or another autobiographical or present consciousness at the time of writing."[1] No single opus in the Ginsberg canon demonstrates that truth better than *Kaddish*. Intimately autobiographical and intensely present in its projection, *Kaddish* is unquestionably Ginsberg at his purest and best.

Because of the raw emotional power of this elegy—its grippingly real evocation of his mother's tortured life and the tortured lives it touched—critics are almost apologetic about discussing it formally as literature. Harvey Shapiro, for instance, suggests that in *Kaddish* Ginsberg "has said what he wanted to say with all the force of his original impulse, and with nothing left out," but that "he had to fight literature to do this."[2] Robert Anton Wilson speaks of Ginsberg's "unpolished-looking verse," and concedes that it requires "three or four readings aloud to feel my way towards Ginsberg's music," acknowledging that his form is "a thing created out of ordinary speech but suddenly, by the height of its emotion, transcending ordinary speech."[3] Emotion, these critics seem to be saying, obviates allegiance to any exterior formal restraints, and like suffering itself, simply dictates its own terms of expression.

Perhaps. But these critics themselves go on to examine the poem formally, taking their lead from *Kaddish*'s opening lines:

. . . I've been up all night, talking, talking, reading Kaddish aloud,
     listening to Ray Charles blues shout blind on the phonograph
the rhythm the rhythm—and your memory in my head three years after—
     And read Adonais' last triumphant stanzas aloud—wept, realizing how
     we suffer—.

(*CP*, 209)

Talking; the Kaddish; Ray Charles; the memory of his mother, Naomi; Adonais—these ingredients, according to Ginsberg himself, constitute the formal matrix from which *Kaddish* grows. We can easily feel the throbbing of the blues cadences, the remembered details of Naomi's suffering, and perhaps—although it has been challenged[4]—the rigor of the Kaddish rite; the contribution of pastoral elegiac form is discernible through *Kaddish*'s allusive procession of mourners but mostly through its remarkable narratives of the poet's intimate association—even identification—with the deceased.

The function of memory as it operates in this elegy is also self-recollection. "I've seen your grave! O strange Naomi!" Ginsberg says, and immediately adds: "My own—cracked grave!" (*CP*, 221). Or in the last section: "Lord Lord Lord Naomi underneath this grass my halflife and my own as her's . . ." (*CP*, 227). History, in this poem, is resuscitated, taken from the tomb of time and given new life, in the "present consciousness."

One has, then, in *Kaddish* a mourner's prayer that oddly contains a distinct pragmatic intention of its own. This mercilessly intimate narrative recollection of the deceased mother becomes the glass through which the poet peers darkly into his own existence. At the same time, because of the inevitable interplay between the confident assurance of "The Mourner's Kaddish" of Reform Judaism and Ginsberg's reworking of the litany, there is great opportunity for irony of the most relevant sort: the irony of the certainty of the official prayer placed against the anguished uncertainty of humanity thrown, in the twentieth century, into a secularized world.

The focal point of this ironic tension centers around the eschatological question that Ginsberg grapples with in such poems as "Metaphysics," "Death, Cannot Reach What is Most Near," and "This is about Death." In *Kaddish*, for example, there is the appeal at the end of section one: "Death, stay thy phantoms!" (*CP*, 212). What this line appears to be is a resolution to refuse all traditional consolations—to face death as finality, to reject the "phantoms" of promises of eternal life; "Blessed be Death on us All!" (*CP*, 225) ends *Kaddish*'s "Hymmnn." In short, Ginsberg's *Kaddish* is an updating of the older, official "Mourner's Kaddish," which cleanses, demythologizes, and denies "the phantoms" of its model. It challenges the relevancy of Judaic eschatological orthodoxy, which avers: "To the departed whom we now remember, may peace and bliss be granted in life eternal. May they find grace and mercy before the Lord of heaven and earth. May their souls rejoice in that ineffable good which God has laid up for those who fear Him, and may their memory be a blessing unto those who treasure it."

The measure of Ginsberg's suspicion of these phantoms of hope is taken early in the poem:

To go where? In that Dark—that—in God? a radiance? A Lord in the Void?
    Like an eye in the black cloud in a dream? Adonoi at last, with you?
Beyond my remembrance! Incapable to guess! Not merely the yellow skull
    in the grave, or a box of worm dust, and a stained ribbon—Deathshead
    with Halo? can you believe it?

                                                                        (CP, 211)

Ginsberg cannot believe; and much of the power of *Kaddish* is generated by the powerful engines of doubt that roar through memory to the final conclusion that "What came is gone forever every time" (CP, 210).

Once the break is made with the "phantoms." the poet is left with the only certain reality he has—himself. *Kaddish* reports this realization, Ginsberg explained on the overleaf of the fifth edition: "These poems almost un-conscious to confess the beatific human fact, the language intuitively chosen as in trance & dream, the rhythms rising from breath into the breast and belly, the hymn completed in tears, the movement of the physical poetry demanding and receiving decades of life while chanting Kaddish the names of Death in many mindworlds the self seeking the Key to life found at last in our self" (CP, 814).

This statement was written in 1963, several years after the composition of the poem; it reflects the shift that had come about in Ginsberg's philosophical posture in Asia during the year documented in "The Change," and provides an exceedingly relevant hindsight to *Kaddish*. Describing the state of mind he was in prior to "The Change," Ginsberg has said that "the psychic problem that I had found myself in was that for various reasons it had seemed to me at one time or another that the best thing to do was to drop dead. Or not be afraid of death but go into death. Go into the non-human, go into the cosmic so to speak; that God was death, and if I wanted to attain God I had to die."[5] This certainly is the attitude underlying *Kaddish* ("Nameless, One Faced, Forever beyond me, beginningless, endless, Father in death" [CP, 212]).

The change that occurred, however, was a distinct deviation from this position, which was anticipated in the tiny cameo poem in *Empty Mirror*:

> I made love to myself
> in the mirror, kissing my own lips,
> saying, "I love myself,
> I love you more than anybody."
>
> (*CP*, 70)

What happened, as Ginsberg describes it, was that "I suddenly didn't want to be *dominated* by that non-human any more, or even be dominated by the moral obligation to enlarge my consciousness any more. . . . I was suddenly free to love myself again, and therefore love people around me, in the form that they already were. And love myself in my own form as I am."[6]

What one finds, therefore, in the comment Ginsberg appends to the fifth edition of *Kaddish*, is a deferred explication de texte, a reinterpretation of a prior intuition in light of a point of view adopted later. It is a verification of poetic prophecy. "What prophecy actually is," Ginsberg feels, "is not that you actually know that the bomb will fall in 1942. It's that you know and feel something which somebody knows and feels in a hundred years. And maybe articulate it in a hint—concrete way that they can pick up on in a hundred years."[7]

Kaddish was written in one long two-day sitting with amphetamine injections "plus a little bit of morphine, plus some dexedrine later on to keep me going." The purpose of the amphetamine, according to Ginsberg, was to give "a peculiar metaphysical tinge to things . . . Space-outs."[8] Although the poem is numerically numbered into five parts, its actual structure includes a "Proem, narrative, hymmnn, lament, litany & fugue." There is little evidence of a serious attempt to follow specifically any of the traditional forms of the Kaddish ritual, but the general rhythmic and procedural similarities are unmistakable. At one point in part two a fragment of "The Mourner's Kaddish" is quoted in Hebrew and inserted in the poem:"*Yisborach, v'yistabach, v'yispoar, v'yisroman, v'yisnaseh, / v'yishador, v'yishalleh, v'yishallol, sh'meh dkudsho, b'rich hu*" (*CP*, 219; May God remember the soul of our honored mother who is gone to her repose).

Repose, in Ginsberg's vocabulary, connotes a merciful salvation from life—relief from "All the accumulations of life that wear us out—clocks, bodies, consciousness, shoes, breasts—begotten sons—your Communism—'Paranoia' into hospitals" (*CP*, 211). As an antonym for life, repose is a scarcely disguised death wish, one that evolves from a weariness, even a disgust, with the "vale of tears" life had become. "We are in a fix!" Ginsberg declares to his dead mother. "And you're out, Death let you out, Death had the Mercy, You're done with your century, done with God, done with the path thru it—Done with yourself at last—Pure—Back to the Babe dark before your Father, before us all—before the world—" (CP, 210). The "consolation" that *Kaddish* offers here is of the same platonic sort we recall from "In Death, Cannot Reach What is Most Near":

> We know all about death . . .
> because we have all experienced
> the state before birth.
>   (CP, 34)

This is no popular heavenly vision; the blessing of death is relief from pain. The triumph over life is stoic forbearance: [There is] Nothing beyond what we have—what you

> had—that so pitiful
> —yet Triumph,
> to have been here, and changed, like a tree, broken, or flower—
> fed to the ground—but mad, with its petals, colored,
> thinking Great Universe, shaken, cut in the head, leaf
> stript, his in an egg crate hospital, cloth wrapped, sore
> —freaked in the moon brain, Naughtless.
>   (CP, 211)

Naomi Ginsberg, the archetype of modernity, has not been tragically cut down suddenly like Emily Dickinson's flower beheaded by "The blond assassin." She is, as Ginsberg notes, "No flower like that flower, which knew itself in the garden, and fought the knife—lost / Cut down by an idiot Snowman's fancy" (CP, 211). Instead, Naomi's demise was slow and tedious, brought on by the dismal accumulations of life that the remainder of the poem documents in stark, horrifying clarity.

As elegy, *Kaddish* voices its protest not against cruel death, but against insane life—or, more to the point, life that drives one insane by its encouragement of mad idealisms and visions of something more. ("The key is in the window, the key is in the sunlight at the window—I have the key—Get married Allen don't take drugs—the key is in the bars, in the sunlight in the window" (CP, 224). [9]

The pathetic, autobiographical narrative of part two requires no explanation. It is the personal diary of a son's witness to his mother's interment under the accumulations of life that wear all to death. It is *"auto*biographical" narrative because the real history presented is not that of Naomi Ginsberg but the history of her son's finding himself in the revitalization of memory; he exploited his recollections of her anguish to help him understand the nature of his own:

> O glorious muse that bore me from the womb, gave
> suck first mystic life and taught me talk and music,
> from whose pained head I first took Vision—
> Tortured and beaten in the skull—What mad
> hallucinations of the damned that drive me out of my
> own skull to seek Eternity till I find Peace for Thee,
> O Poetry—and for all humankind call on the Origin.
>
> *(CP,* 223)

The "mad hallucinations of the damned" that Ginsberg speaks of are not a rhetorical extravagance but an acknowledgment of an actual autobiographical experience—his Blake vision. Much of the material in *Kaddish* is directly related to this crucial phenomenon in Ginsberg's life because the experience opened a new level of consciousness to the poet, permitting him to glimpse the possibility of the radical oneness of the world and existence. Using a phrase from Blake's poem "The Little Girl Lost" ("Then let Lyca wake"), Ginsberg asks himself: ". . . wake to what? *Wake* meaning wake to . . . [the] existence in the entire universe. . . . In other words a breakthrough from ordinary habitual quotidian consciousness into consciousness that was really seeing all of heaven in a flower."[10]

At another point he calls this "a sudden awakening into a totally deeper real universe than I'd been existing in." The psychological result of this vision is a split consciousness—a double vision of the world, or roughly the equivalent of appreciating a noumenal as well as a phenomenal existence. The appeal of Naomi's cryptic advice "The key is in the window" undoubtedly was its unwitting relevance to Ginsberg's Blake vision: "Looking out the window," he has said, "through the window at the sky, suddenly it seemed that I saw into the depths of the universe, by looking simply into the ancient sky. . . . And this was the very ancient place that he was talking about, the sweet golden clime, I suddenly realized that *this* existence was *it*!"[11] It is only natural that such an experience should exploit religious language for adequate expression.

Kaddish documents the horror of a universe that has lost its integrity, its knowledge of the oneness of all selves. Madness is the metaphor, and not just the madness of Naomi and Allen, but the question of the very authenticity of madness. Is it madness to see the universe on a different level of reality from Ginsberg or Naomi? The problem is recorded in *Howl*: "Who thought they were only mad when Baltimore gleamed in supernatural ecstasy" (*CP*, 127). "If it were only that easy!" says Ginsberg by way of explanation. "In other words it'd be a lot easier if you just were crazy, instead of—then you could chalk it up, 'well I'm nutty'—but on the other hand what if it's all true and you're *born* into this great cosmic universe in which you're a spirit angel."[12]

There is an equation in *Kaddish* between insight into a deeper consciousness of the universe and an allusion to God or the Creator. Ginsberg gave the deeper consciousness a "holy Name." Hence, in the "Hymmnn" of *Kaddish*, the "He" who is praised is a highly ambivalent entity. "He" is not all an orthodox deity, but existence—Being—itself. But even this is not a sufficient definition, for it is not abstract ontology that Ginsberg makes reference to here; it is to a personalized human Being—sentient awareness of existential solidarity; meaning that, indeed, "No man is an island unto himself" and one can see all of heaven in a flower.

Part four of *Kaddish* ends with the line addressed to Naomi "with your Death full of Flowers" (*CP*, 227), another indication that the flower symbol is of paramount significance in Ginsberg's poetry. It seems to have found its priority in Ginsberg's hierarchy of values because of its relation to the Blake vision. For Ginsberg was reading Blake's "The Sick Rose" when "the voice" spoke to him. While confessing that he cannot explain it on a verbal level, Ginsberg remarks, "The sick rose is myself or self, or the living body, sick because the mind, which is the worm 'that flies in the night, in the howling storm' . . . is destroying it, or let us say death, the worm as being death, the natural process of death, some kind of mystical being of its own trying to come in and devour the body, the rose."[13]

The broadly tentative equation between the worm, the mind, and death corresponds suggestively with William Blake's four "Zoas" or "classical divisions" alluded to in Chapter Two, from which, we recall, Ginsberg concluded that "reason has become a 'horrific tyrant' in Western civilization and created the nuclear bomb which can destroy body, feeling and intimidate and all but destroy imagination."[14]

"Hymmnn" ends with the words "Blessed be Death on us all" (*CP*, 225), which reinforces *Kaddish*'s consolation for the dead with a theme suggestive of Wallace Stevens's in "Sunday Morning":

> Death is the mother of beauty; hence from her,
> Alone, shall come fulfillment to our dreams
> And our desires.

Ginsberg adds a characteristic twist to his version of the notion: "If you get interested in Beauty, then you've latched onto something mysterious inside your soul that grows and grows like a secret insane thought, and takes over completely when you die, and you're IT."

Not only is death a release from the "mechano-universe of unfeeling Time," but it is also an inevitable yielding to that mysterious, "secret insane thought" inside one's soul. The higher level of consciousness that sees the cosmos in timelessness provides a perspective that extracts fear from the mystery of death: "all Earth one everlasting Light in the familiar blackout—no tears for this vision," says Ginsberg toward the end of part three.

> But that the key should be left behind—at the window—the key in the
>   sunlight—to the living—that can take
> that slice of light in hand—and turn the door—and look back see
> Creation glistening backwards to the same grave, size of universe, size of the
>   tick of the hospital's clock on the archway over the white door. . . .
>
>   (*CP*, 226)

"Madness as metaphor" controls the whole of part four. The terrifying bifurcation of Naomi's existence—sliced in the middle by double vision, seeing the world and seeing the universe simultaneously, and being pulled apart by the tension into insanity—is rendered through the ambivalence of the anchor phrase "with your eyes." This catalogue is one of horrors; the biological attrition to death in the final lines underscores graphically not so much the "*accumulations* of life, that wear us out," but the pitiful *reductio ad nihilum* of a human being. The potentiality of the word *eyes* as homonym serves to universalize a particular, terrifying biography. It is not only Naomi's "eyes running naked out of the apartment screaming into the hall," but the "I's" of us all. One might even find in these lines the "Ayes" of one's consent.

Beyond Mind Consciousness

The final page of *Kaddish and Other Poems* contains the following
note: "Magic Psalm, The Reply, & The End *record visions experienced
after drinking Ayahuasca, an Amazon spiritual potion. The message is:
Widen the area of consciousness.*"[15] While only these three poems are
cited as examples of trance notations, many of the other poems in the
volume deal with the relevancy of the counsel *"Widen the area of consciousness."* The possibility of multiple levels of consciousness and
planes of reality beyond normal rational limits became real to Ginsberg when Blake spoke to him in Harlem, but such possibilities have,
of course, been known since prehistory. Erich Fromm, for example,
has described the human being as "tormented by a craving for 'abso-
luteness,' for another kind of harmony which can lift the curse by
which he was separated from nature, from his fellow men, and from
himself."[16] Theologian Paul Tillich observes that "man is finite . . .
but man is also aware of his potential infinity."[17] Ginsberg's comment
on the phenomenon is partially articulated in "Laughing Gas":

> It's the instant of going
> into or coming out of
> existence that is
> important—to catch on
> to the secret of the magic
>   box
>
> Stepping outside the universe
>   by means of Nitrous Oxide
> anesthetizing mind-consciousness. . . .
>   (*CP*, 189)

What is at stake here cannot be exhausted completely by the term
mysticism, but it certainly partakes of mysticism's intention to probe
beyond what Ginsberg calls "mind consciousness." Traditional mystics—the purists—must be suspicious, as Ginsberg eventually is himself,[18] of biochemical assaults upon the ineffable; and "Laughing Gas"
certainly documents the perils of narcotic undiscipline in such ventures. Real mystics might shake their heads knowingly at Ginsberg's
frustration in finding the mind "an irrational traffic light in Gobi"
(*CP*, 191), but they would certainly assent to his proposition that

> The universe is a void
> in which there is a dreamhole
> The dream disappears
>   the hole closes.
>
> (*CP*, 189)

Mystic experience is transient, for the hole is always closing. The glimpse is all that can be hoped for; but, once the glimpse has been seen, the soul seeks a repeat performance. So unbearable is the desire for Ginsberg that his life becomes committed to a constant quest through whatever avenues he finds at hand. For a significant portion of his career, drugs served the purpose. In answer to the question if his use of drugs was an extension of his Blake experience, Ginsberg replied: "drugs were obviously a technique for experimenting with consciousness, to get different areas and different levels and different similarities and different reverberations of the same vision. . . . There are certain moments under laughing gas and aether that the consciousness does intersect with something similar—for me—to my Blake visions."[19]

There is a connection, therefore, among a majority of the poems in the *Kaddish* volume, which can roughly be described as attempts to induce mystic flights. The place to begin an examination of this connection is the poem "The Lion for Real," which is an allegorical presentation of Ginsberg's original Blake vision. The poem version of the experience itself adds little that has not been dealt with in Ginsberg's prose accounts except that the objectification of the "voice" into animal form has the effect of focusing the emotional power of the vision into an awesome, even savage, intensity. "Terrible Presence!" the poet cries, "Eat me or die!" (*CP*, 175). A frightening dimension of newly perceived reality is confronted. Theologically, the experience falls under the Judeo-Christian concept of the "wrath of God"; Ginsberg's reaction to it reflects a similar sense of cosmic threat: "[The lion] said in a gravelly voice 'Not this time Baby—but I will be back again'" (*CP*, 175).

One cannot escape the religious depth of the event as it is depicted in verse. Donne's famous holy sonnet comes immediately to mind:

> Batter my heart, three person'd God for you
> As yet but knocke, breathe, shine and seeke to mend,

That I may rise, and stand, o'erthrow mee, and bend
Your force, to breake, blowe, burn and make me new. . . .
                                                                          for I
Except you enthrall mee, never shall be free,
Nor ever chaste, except you ravish mee.[20]

Ginsberg's poem contains no petition to the "Terrible Presence" other
than the appeal to do his worst ("Eat me or die!") and get it over
with; but the power of the Presence is acknowledged as a God, and
that power is irresistible:

Lion that eats my mind now for a decade knowing only your hunger
Not the bliss of your satisfaction O roar of the Universe how am I chosen
In this life I have heard your promise I am ready to die I have served
Your starved and ancient Presence O Lord I wait in my room at your Mercy.
                                                                          (CP, 175)

The Presence is a sadistic demon. Like the "Cruel Fair" of Petrarch's
sonnets, it attracts but never offers satisfaction. The victimized devo-
tee starvingly awaits the dubious promise of mercy.

The anguish of worshiping such a Presence is provoked by the fact
of its transiency. It is a mystic glimpse—"Just a flash in the cosmic
pan"—and there is no certitude of its authenticity. "The whole universe a shaggy dog story! with a weird ending that begins again till
you get the point . . ." (CP, 191). Worse, there may be no point at
all:

An endless cycle of possibilities clashing in Nothing
with each mistake in the writing inevitable from the beginning of time
The doctor's phone number is Pilgrim 1–0000
Are you calling me, Nothing?
                                                                          (CP, 195)

Ginsberg, as pilgrim, is faced with the dizzy possibilities of nothing-
ness—a classic existentialist situation that calls for something akin to
the Kierkegaardian "leap of faith." Hence, one has his "decade knowing only [the lion's] hunger" (CP, 175).

Thus, "The Lion for Real" inevitably leads in Kaddish to "Laughing
Gas," and "Laughing Gas" to "Mescaline," "Lysergic Acid," "Magic
Psalm," "The Reply," and "The End," all poems that reflect the at-
tempt at consciousness expansion through drugs that the lion seems

to demand. Ginsberg later referred to these poems as "records of bum trips" in which he was "still looking for a vision, trying to superimpose the acid vision on the old memory of a cosmic-consciousness, or to superimpose an old memory on the acid vision—so that I was not living in the present time, not noticing so much of what was in front of me."[21]

It was a wild and often unpleasant pilgrimage, but pilgrimage it was, even literally, for it took Ginsberg to the outlands of Peru in search of *yage*, the drug to end drugs. "Thank you, O Lord, beyond my eye," he says in "Mescaline," "the path must lead somewhere . . ." (*CP*, 228).

Poem as Prayer

"Magic Psalm" is particularly intriguing because of its apparent kinship with the poems of spiritual anguish that we have come to associate with Donne, Herbert, and Hopkins. "Magic Psalm"'s indebtedness to the Donne sonnet quoted above is strikingly evident:

Drive me crazy, God I'm ready for disintegration of my mind, disgrace me
    in the eye of the earth,
attack my hairy heart with terror . . . leap on me pack of heavy dogs
    salivating light,
devour my brain . . .
Descend O Light Creator & Eater of Mankind, disrupt the world in its
    madness of bombs and murder. . . .

                        (*CP*, 256)

Perhaps even more informative is the device of the naming of "God" that Ginsberg uses as his metrical anchor. The poem begins with a long catalogue of evocations that is so comprehensive that soon a cumulative suggestion of what Ginsberg means by the "Terrible Presence" begins to emerge. He is called:

O Phantom that my mind pursues from year to year . . .
Giant outside Time . . .
Unspeakable King of the roads that are gone . . .
Unintelligible Horse riding out of the graveyard . . .
Griever . . . Laugh with no mouth, Heart that never had flesh to die—
    Promise that was not made . . .
Reliever . . . Destroyer of the World . . . Creator of Breasted Illusions. . . .

                        (*CP*, 255)

To this Being, a petition is made in various forms to disrupt personal rationality ("devour my brain"), as well as the corporate rationality of civilization, identified as evil ("disrupt the world in its madness of bombs and murder" (*CP*, 256).

As prayer, the poem directs its appeals most significantly to "Beauty invisible to my century!" (*CP*, 256) and asks this deity for the power to evoke a prayer that passes even the author's understanding. This prayer then unfolds, toward the end of the poem, into a series of specific requests that probe to the very core of Ginsberg's concern:

that I surpass desire for transcendency and enter the calm water of the
    universe
that I ride out this wave, not drown forever in the flood of my imagination
that I not be slain thru my own insane magic. . . .

                                                                    (*CP*, 256)

This triad of petitions outlines Ginsberg's dilemma. The first suggests his need for peace, for the decade of pilgrimage initiated by the Blake vision has worn him down. The mad quest for the transcendent, which was also the fate of Naomi, is seen as a destructive force within him that must be overcome. Peace must be made with the universe and with existence; quite possibly, the serenity of the Tao is the true object of the appeal.

The second petition is a call for help from a man drowning in his own imagination. His thoughts are torments that lead him he knows not where. The third request follows accordingly that death be not the outcome of his "insane magic." Precisely what this "insane magic" is, is Ginsberg's alleged God-given mission to prophesy, which becomes evident in a final appended appeal that

    men understand my speech out of their own Turkish heart,
    the prophets aid me with Proclamation,
    the Seraphim acclaim Thy Name, Thyself at once in one huge
    Mouth of Universe make meat reply.

                                                                    (*CP*, 256)

Under the influence of *ayahuasca* the messianic energy latent in Ginsberg is given full vent, and the appeal is dramatically underscored by the imperative demand for an answer: "make meat reply."

The pun is a happy fruit of invention that combines the urgency of the poet's need for a proper answer to his prayer with a suggestion as to the appropriate idiom: through "meat"—the flesh, the humanity, the "sensate transcendency" (*CP*, 255) of the divine essence. This term also corresponds with the earlier request that the Phantom "invade my body with the sex of God" (*CP*, 255).

"The Reply," the companion piece to "Magic Psalm," can be properly appreciated only after digesting the factual account of Ginsberg's experimentation with *ayahuasca*, which he gives in all its terrifying detail in a letter to William Burroughs. The effect of this drug was, in Ginsberg's words, "the strongest and worst I've ever had it nearly—(I still reserve the Harlem experiences, being natural, in abeyance."[22] The fear that saturates the letter (so great that Ginsberg feels compelled to assure Burroughs at the close that "everything is OK, I suppose, in case this all just worries you unnecessarily, I'll be all right") is the fear of a man confronting death. "I felt faced by Death," he wrote to Burroughs; the emotion is poetically transcribed into the opening line of the poem as "God answers with my doom!" (*CP*, 257).

As in most experiences of fear, the triggering ingredient is the unknown:

> I am a Seraph and I know not whither I go into the Void
> I am a man and I know not whither I go into Death—
> Christ Christ poor hopeless
> lifted on the Cross between Dimension—
> to see the Ever-Unknowable!
> (*CP*, 257)

The poem advances little toward a solution of Ginsberg's basic eschatological problem. Bede's ancient metaphor of the swallow in flight through the brief light of the illuminated hall still encompasses the dilemma. The emotional volume of the poet's response to it is drastically intensified in this poem by the "mind-expanding" properties of the drug. Even the problem of illusion versus reality is deliberately swept aside by Ginsberg in order to meet the experience head-on. "I was frightened," he explained to Burroughs, "and simply lay there with wave after wave of death-fear, fright, rolling over me till I could hardly stand it, didn't want to take refuge in rejecting it as illusion, for it was too real and too familiar."[23]

As seraph or as person, the fear of "the Void" seems inescapable. The poem appears to document the frenzy of a man who has lifted his head above the waves of temporality expecting to find a "peace which passeth all understanding," but who finds instead the more terrifying cipher of annihilation. "I am annulled" (CP, 257), he discovers in "The Reply"; and almost immediately he identifies his experience with Christ who has almost shared his hopeless feeling of being "lifted on the Cross between Dimension" (CP, 257).

So much, then, for divine transcendence; for "What's sacred when the Thing is all the universe?" (CP, 258). The horrible predicament lies in the fact that there is indeed no exit: "No refuge in Myself, which is on fire / or in the World which is His also to bomb & devour!" (CP, 258). The "faceless Destroyer," which the vision of God has revealed, is malignantly omnipotent; and the poem ends on the most pessimistic of notes: "The universe turns inside out to devour me! / and the mighty burst of music comes from out the inhuman door—" (CP, 258).

Faced with such a dead end, it is inevitable that consolation must come from within; and the concluding poem of the volume, appropriately titled "The End," seems to herald this message, if in muted tones. The counterreply to "the Thing" is the simple declaration: "I am I, old Father Fisheye that begat the ocean, the worm at my own ear . . ." (CP, 259). From this premise follows the humanistic bravado of one uneasily balancing a cosmic chip on his shoulder: "I receive all, I'll die of cancer, I enter the coffin forever, / I close my eye, I disappear . . ." (CP, 259). This shaky assertion is bolstered by the familiar standby—Love:

Love that bore me I bear back to my Origin with no loss, I float over the
     vomiter
thrilled with my deathlessness, thrilled with this endlessness. . . .

                                                                                    (CP, 259)

Curiously, however, the "thrill" of "deathlessness" has no observable source in the poem. The optimistic tag rings hollow, despite an apparantly postscriptive appeal to aesthetics as the key to the eschatological problem: "come Poet shut up eat my word, and taste my mouth in your ear" (CP, 259). The resolution to this problem is not to be bought so cheaply; it requires a trip to Asia, talks with holy men from India, and a conversation with Martin Buber. On this trip

Ginsberg learns that the true focus of the difficulty lies in the area of "human relationships rather than relations between the human and the non-human."[24] Hence, in 1963, Ginsberg adds the comment on the flyleaf of *Kaddish*: "the Key to life found at last in our self."

Whatever keys people have found to unlock the doors to existence have traditionally been sought and found in the ideas of God as an entity. Clearly, Ginsberg's courtship with drugs served to objectify an inherent religious need into various magnified entities that reveal themselves as "Terrible Presences" or "Devourers." By taking the option of choosing self over a God-entity, Ginsberg has accomplished what might be called a transition from a transcendent view of deity toward an existential one. In other words, God-as-entity has proved to be a psychological cul-de-sac; or, as Ginsberg puts it more specifically, "The Asian experience kind of got me out of the corner I painted myself in with drugs."[25] Drugs had taken him as far as he could go in his quest for an objectified God; they had brought him to terror and despair. The final lines of "The End"—"come Poet shut up eat my word, and taste my mouth in your ear"—suggest a new start. The God-entity—the "Terrible Presence"—is supplanted by a more negotiable conception of God as Being. The "I am I" of the first line seems a commitment to existence in its inchoate stage, and this commitment permits Ginsberg to maintain at least one of his feet in the practical world of the here-and-now.

Van Gogh and Aunt Rose

An earlier poem, "Death to Van Gogh's Ear!" shows how effective Ginsberg can be with clipped wings. The theme is familiar: the usual list of atrocities committed against humanity in the name of "The American Way of Life." The title itself serves as the overlying metaphor: Van Gogh's ear, sliced off by the painter to please a prostitute, is a symbol of irrational, unorthodox behavior, but at the same time is an ultimate human gesture of love. There is a conspiracy against such insane acts which betray the hidden, yet essential, humanity of all people, Ginsberg feels. Hence, the whimsical appeal that America put "Van Gogh's Ear on the currency" (*CP*, 169). The implication is, of course, that the ear is a more viable guide to America's self-realization than "In God We Trust." The creative artist (Van Gogh) is placed in competition with God as the guide to a fitting destiny, and so the poem opens with the assertion: "Poet is Priest."

If the poets are priests, their function is to listen to the confessions of the nation. All the confessions that follow in catalogue point to one spiritual disease, which is prediagnosed in the second line: "Money has reckoned the soul of America." The rest of the poem is a frenzied complaint centering on the agonizing disparity between the ideal and the real, the human and the inhuman, the spiritual and the material. "The American Century" has been "betrayed by a mad Senate which no longer sleeps with its wife" (CP, 167). Government and institutions in general have outgrown love. America is impotent; it is "lacklove."

Industry also comes under the priestly wrath: "Detroit has built a million automobiles of rubber trees and phantoms / but I walk, I walk, and the Orient walks with me, and all Africa walks" (CP, 167). Trees become machines, and people become parts of machines that no longer walk. Only the Priest himself and Orient (the mind of Tao?) remain bipeds. The tremendous fertility of America is reduced to barrenness—"mountains of eggs were reduced to white powder in the halls of Congress"—while the rest of the world goes hungry:

aborigines of Australia perhaps gibber in the eggless wilderness
and I rarely have an egg for breakfast tho my work requires infinite eggs to
      come to birth in Eternity
eggs should be eaten or given to their mothers. . . .

                                                                    (CP, 167)

The poem rises in a crescendo of anger culminating in an outburst that echoes the Moloch section of *Howl*:

Money! Money! Money! shrieking mad celestial money of illusion! Money
      made of nothing, starvation, suicide! Money of failure Money of death!
Money against Eternity! and eternity's strong mills grind out vast paper of
      Illusion!

                                                                    (CP, 170)

Nothing more needs to be said except for the usual reminder from Ginsberg that he is the voice of the prophet: "History will make this poem prophetic and its awful silliness a / hideous spiritual music . . ." (CP, 168).

When the poems in *Kaddish* are not "hideous spiritual music," they often draw on a source of poignant power that proves consistently more reliable than mystic vision. Because they are less pretentious and seemingly less ambitious, they often, as if by accident, hit a chord of such personal intimacy that they sing to the muse of pure poetry. "To Aunt Rose" is one such poem. It is Ginsberg's "Portrait of a Woman" made rich, like the collection as a whole, by self-discovering memory. It requires no explanation because it is the simple rendering of a woman. An entire existence is somehow evoked with an amazing economy of remembered glimpses and reconstructed insights, each of which is in itself almost capable of capturing the essence of Aunt Rose:

> . . . your tears of sexual frustration
> (what smothered sobs and bony hips
> under the pillows of Osborne terrace).
>
> (*CP*, 184)

What separates "To Aunt Rose" from the poems of trance notation is the simple element of control. In the former, admiration is inspired by the confidence that there is a maker behind the poem—that a keen, perceptive discrimination has presented the precise details necessary for capturing a delicate subtlety. The trance notations do not do this. It is not maker but transcriber who overwhelms the reader with the sound and fury of infinitude. Relative to this observation is Karl Shapiro's conviction that "the poet's rapport with God is relatively crude and is like that of the magician and the psychologist rather than that of the mystic. For the poet, the unitive experience is forever blocked by the nature of creative work, art being an embodiment of personality and not a surrender of personality to the larger Being."[26]

Chapter Six
Reality Sandwiches

The Menu

"On Burroughs' Work" concludes with the stanza

> A naked lunch is natural to us,
>   we eat reality sandwiches.
> But allegories are so much lettuce.
> Don't hide the madness.
>   (*CP*, 114)

The title of this fourth volume of collected poems thus pays homage to two of Ginsberg's most influential friends: Jack Kerouac, who suggested *Naked Lunch* as an appropriate title for Burroughs's novel, and, of course, Burroughs himself. Burroughs contends that "[*Naked Lunch*] means exactly what the words say: NAKED Lunch—a frozen moment when everyone sees what is on the end of every fork."[1] *Reality Sandwiches* presumes to exhibit twenty-nine such "frozen moments" that span seven years of Ginsberg's development (1953–60).

Both Ginsberg's and Burroughs's titles promise readers a taste of pure reality and demand that they savor its sweetness and bitterness with a vital palate. Both writers presume to serve an existential feast devoid of hypocritical condiments that might disguise "the madness." In both cases, the program is ambitious and suggests the radical, synesthetic entreaty that Ginsberg once made to Peter Orlovsky when he dedicated *Kaddish and Other Poems* to him: "Taste my mouth in your ear."

The reader gets a good taste of Ginsberg's mouth in this collection, which, as usual, is uninhibitedly and often flamboyantly honest. As a poetic method, unadulterated honesty is hardly a new departure for Ginsberg. In real life honesty had led him to jail sentences, obscenity trials, and a "second-rate creep image that was interpreted to the public via mass media."[2] Honesty also led to the lonely regions of isolation where death and self struggle to negotiate a viable program of being. There is much discussion in these poems of what Heidegger called the "authentic" versus the "inauthentic" life, as well as some further jousting with the problem of death. The menu is varied and the service erratic; but, true to his word, Ginsberg is sparing with the lettuce in his sandwiches and the taste of madness is strong.

Illuminations

The initial poem, "My Alba," is an experiment within traditional forms that bears, as so many of Ginsberg's early verses, a strong resemblance to Williams's style. The subject is wasted time, and the method is the catalogue. Williams's poem *"Le Médecin malgré Lui"* might easily stand as the model; but Ginsberg thrusts beyond its structural ennui to arrive at a description of a human being poised for a spring into authentic existence. It is a morning song that anticipates an awakening. The poet seems to be undergoing the shock of discovering that his life has been nonbeing; his metaphor is the paraphernalia of the business office. His life is not measured in coffee spoons, but worse:

> Sliderule and number
> machine on a desk
> autographed triplicate
> synopsis and taxes. . . .

This catalogue documents a wasted "five years in Manhattan / life decaying / talent a blank."

Ginsberg's technique is successful in that a sense of boredom is created by the incessant run-on lines and by the complete avoidance of any punctuation. The result is an abundance of suggestive liaisons, which occur between thought patterns: "Manhattan / life decaying . . . blank / talking disconnected / patient . . . mental / sliderule." The feeling that Ginsberg creates and sustains by the use and the structure of language in the body of the poem is decisive in making possible the structural tension that the title lends to the entire poem. The juxtaposition of the awakening, implicit in the title "My Alba," with the ostentatiously banal poem that follows is an example of Ginsberg's borrowing of Williams's typical method of creating significance from structure.

As reinforcement to the structural significance of the poem, Ginsberg also adds a final note of existential urgency: "I am damned to Hell what / alarmclock is ringing." By this time, the reader realizes that the preceding stanzas have attempted to chart the precincts of hell and that the ringing of the alarm clock is the sudden awareness of a crisis. The "autographed triplicate / synopsis" is a carbon copy existence; it is inauthentic, and it is time to awaken to a naked breakfast.

The penultimate stage of illumination that this poem suggests reminds the reader of traditional experiences of religious regeneration in which one is "reborn" to a new understanding of existence. The second selection, a Zen poem called "Sakyamuni Coming Out from the Mountain," takes its title from a scroll painting by Liang K'ai that, as Ginsberg tells us, "showed Sakyamuni Buddha with long, tearful eyebrows and big ears, looking as if he's been on the mountain a long ascetic year and had experienced a comedown enlightenment of some kind."[3] The poem addresses the difficulty of being twice-born:

> how painful to be born again
> wearing a fine beard,
> reentering the world.
>
> (CP, 90)

The form of this poem again seems derivative from Williams's experiments with the three-step, variable foot line in *Paterson, Desert Music,* and *Journey to Love.* A single specimen from *Paterson II* suffices to illustrate the similarity:

> The descent beckons
>   as the ascent beckoned
>   Memory is a kind
> of accomplishment
>   a sort of renewal
>   even
> an initiation. . . .[4]

The characteristics of this style are that each of the three steps is intended to be equal and that, after each step down, there is a caesural pause. The effect is rather like syncopation; the lines come, as John Ciardi suggests, just "off the beat" of iambic pentameter, and they follow the general rhythmic patterns of modern jazz.[5] For Williams the method was "a way of escaping the formlessness of free verse," and the intention was also presumably Ginsberg's.[6] At the same time, however, Ginsberg was concerned that the poem have an oriental flavor; and one could easily make a case for the form's congeniality with haiku.

Liang-k'ai was a painter of the Sung dynasty (957–1279), and his work represents a reciprocal relationship between humans and nature. In other words, his landscapes depict "a world to which man belongs but which he does not dominate."[7] The attitude does much to explain the final declaration of Ginsberg's poem: "humility is beatness / before the absolute World," which in turn reflects Heidegger's thesis that the human predicament is that people have been "thrown" into a world with which they must come to terms. Hence, the poem is rich in the philosophical possibilities that emerge from a matrix of Taoism, Zen, beatness, and existentialism.

The theme of the aimless life, so characteristic of Zen thought, is presented in the opening description of Arhat who

> drags his bare feet
> out of a cave . . .
> wearing a fine beard,
> unhappy hands
> clasped to his naked breast . . . faltering
> into the bushes by a stream.
>
> (*CP*, 90)

The issue of the connection between humans and nature is then introduced: "all things inanimate / but his intelligence." The function of the intelligence according to Zen is not to separate one from nature but to perform as a receptor of momentary glimpses into authentic Being that testify to one's oneness with the world. Humility (beatness) begins to emerge in the reader's mind as a state engendering the realization that one is nothing special in the face of the "absolute World." This recognition seems to be the denouement that the narrative poem offers.

Arhat has been seeking Heaven "under a mountain of stone," and in typical Zen fashion he has "sat thinking" (not imposing his thoughts upon nature, but passively awaiting an understanding) until an awakening occurs. He realizes that "the hand of blessedness exists / in the imagination." This realization is analogous to the ringing of an alarm clock, and Arhat is reborn; his "inauthentic" existence is authenticated and he is made humble:

> he knows nothing
>   like a god:
>   shaken
> meek wretch—.
>   (*CP*, 90–91)

In essence, Ginsberg's poem supplies an answer to one of the fundamental questions existentialism poses: "are we disclosed to ourselves as existents who are always already in a world—a world with which we are concerned and involved in all kinds of ways—so that it is out of this total situation that we must seek after whatever understanding of Being may be possible for us; or are we, as the traditional Western philosophy had been inclined to regard us, primarily thinking subjects, before whom there is spread out for our inspection a world, and this world is to be understood in a genuine way only along the lines of detached theoretical inquiry?"[8] Clearly, "beatness" or "humility" understands only the first option.

"Over Kansas" is another poem that describes a similar illumination, but a contemporary American backdrop replaces the misty forests and lonely rocks of the Sung landscape painters. The situation of the poem is an airplane journey across the United States, one that becomes, in the poet's consciousness, a subjective journey from egoless nonbeing, through a vision of Kansas at night, to a form of self-realization. Two implicit themes embrace in the consummation of this poem: death and nakedness. Death haunts the stanzas in the several references to "death insurance by machine" (*CP*, 117) and the hypothetical poet below in Kansas who is "Someone who should collect / my insurance!" (*CP*, 119). More profoundly, however, death enters the meditations of the traveler as he ponders the fact that he is

> Travelling thru the dark void
> over Kansas yet moving nowhere
> in the dark void of the soul.
>   (*CP*, 118)

Death is also present in his mind when he muses that

> Not even the human
> imagination satisfied
> the endless emptiness of the soul.
>   (*CP*, 117)

Then comes the official illumination over Hutchinson, Kansas, where the poet peers beyond his own reflection in the window ("bald businessman with hornrims") and sees a "spectral skeleton of electricity"

> illuminated nervous system
> floating on the void out
> of central brainplant powerhouse
> running into heaven's starlight
> overhead.
>
> (*CP,* 118)

The vision is an emblem, presumably. The lights of Hutchinson emanating out of a "central brainplant powerhouse" (the human mind) "floating on the void." Because this "illuminated nervous system" is seen by the poet to be "running into heaven's starlight / overhead, " it seems apparent that "the vision" reveals the potentiality of the human imagination to connect the heavens and this world—in a word, mysticism.

What the reader is up against, then, is the familiar credo of the angel "hipster." "It'd be a lot easier if you just were crazy," Ginsberg has said, ". . . but on the other hand what if it's all true and you're *born* into this great cosmic universe in which you're a spirit angel . . . ?"[9] After the illumination, the poet is in Chicago between flights and decides that this city is "another project for the heart.":

> six months for here someday
> to make Chicago natural,
> pick up a few strange images.
>
> (*CP,* 118)

This spirit angel is on the lookout for missionary work, and it begins to come clear that "nakedness" refers to the condition of unaccommodated humans who find in their misery that all are brothers under the skin, that all are angels. In Ginsberg's world, unauthenticated angels rarely fly; their feet trod the dusty earth where life takes place:

> Better I make
> a thornful pilgrimage on theory
> feet to suffer the total
> isolation of the bum,

> than this hipster
> business family journey
> —crossing U.S. at night—.
>
> (*CP*, 119)

There are so many complex constituents to Ginsberg's illumination that it is often difficult to analyze or even comprehend precisely the response that is expected. The fact that Ginsberg himself often confesses that he is usually not aware of exactly what he means at the time of writing lends little comfort.[10] Nevertheless, even when exegesis fails, communication of a sort often breaks through. Graffiti collectors are reported to have uncovered this interesting specimen in a men's lavatory: "Ginsberg revises!" If the legend were true, perhaps the task of the explicator would be simplified. For good or for bad, Ginsberg does not write for expositors but for angels; and one must be alert to Wordsworth's counsel that "we murder to dissect."

"Sather Gate Illumination" may not present as many problems as "Over Kansas," but the honest lyricism of its celebration of a moment in space and in time manages to avoid the straining for effect that many of the poems in *Reality Sandwiches* exhibit. The poem is Whitman-inspired through and through from the gracious tribute in the beginning ("Dear Walter, thanks for the message" [*CP*, 142]) to the illumination proper at the end: "Seeing in people the visible evidence of inner self thought by their treatment of me: who loves himself loves me who love myself" (*CP*, 145). Almost any line picked at random from *Song of Myself* serves to explicate the general theme of Ginsberg's piece:

> I CELEBRATE myself, and sing myself,
> And what I assume you shall assume,
> For every atom belonging to me as good belongs to you.

Or

> There was never any more inception than there is now,
> Nor any more youth or age than there is now,
> And will never be any more perfection than there is now,
> Nor any more heaven or hell than there is now.

Even more informative are the lines

Clear and sweet is my soul, and clear and sweet is all that is not my soul
Lack one lacks both, and the unseen is proved by the seen,
Till that becomes unseen and receives proof in its turn.[11]

"Dear Walter"'s message is no stopgap communiqué for Ginsberg,
but a program of positive perception as well as a healthy dose of self-
vindication. It reaffirms the brotherhood of angels: "Why do I deny
manna to another? / Because I deny it to myself" (*CP*, 142). The key
to the illumination is the acceptance of self that the poem affirms
from the start:

Now I believe you are lovely, my soul, soul of Allen, Allen—
and you so beloved, so sweetened, so recalled to your true loveliness,
your original nude breathing Allen
will you ever deny another again?"

(*CP*,   142)

There is precious little that is new in the content of this poem; its
effect probably rests on the fact that the poet's mind has been liber-
ated for mere observation. A dazzling array of commonplace scenes
and incidents are raised to significance by the slender support of
Whitman's insight and buttressed by poetic sensitivity. Moral tension
is structurally built into the poem by the leitmotif of the "Roar again
of airplanes in the sky" whose pilots "are sweating and nervous at the
controls in the hot cabins" (*CP*, 142). These bombers with their
"loveless bombs" perform as a mobile umbrella shadowing both the
giggling girls, "all pretty / every-whichway," and the crippled lady,
who "explains French grammar with a loud sweet voice: / Regarder is
to look."
     Looking is the genius of this poem, and it is not only the "scato-
logical insight"[12] that Ginsberg's eye exploits as he observes the "pel-
vic energy" of the crippled girl's bouncing body, but the deeper
vision of the "unseen" being "proved by the seen." Professor Hart,
"enlightened by the years," walks "through the doorway and arcade
he built (in his mind) / and knows—he too saw the ruins of Yucatan
once—" (*CP*, 143). The unseen that the poet reveals through his perception surely is the sense of community that binds humanity together: "we all look up," Ginsberg observes, "silence moves, huge
changes upon the ground, and in the air thoughts fly all over filling
space" (*CP*, 144).

The salutary moment is both spiritual and poetic. "My grief at Peter's not loving me was grief at not loving myself," the poet concludes. Minds that are broken in "beautiful bodies [are] unable to
receive love because not knowing the self as lovely." The illumination
is no less poignant because it derives from Whitman. Indeed, from
Whitman the poetic impulse behind the creation becomes much
clearer; for, in the words of the "True American," Walt Whitman,
Ginsberg's literary foundation can be seen:

> I know I am solid and sound
> To me the converging objects of the universe perpetually flow,
> All are written to me, and I must get what the writing means.[13]

Love and Nakedness

The doctrine of "nakedness" that Ginsberg continually preaches is
implicit in "Sather Gate Illumination"; and it, too, owes much to
Whitman. "Undrape! you are not guilty to me, not stale not dis-
card," one reads in *Song of Myself*:

> I see through the broadcloth and gingham whether or no
> And am around, tenacious, acquisitive, tireless, and cannot
> be shaken away.[14]

Clothes are not only a hindrance to lovemaking; they are the garments
of illusion with which people shamefully hide their humanity. Mind,
too often, is the grim tailor, which appears to be one of the underlying themes of "Love Poem on Theme by Whitman." In this poem,
the poet shares the nuptial bed of "the bridegroom and the bride" of
humanity whose "bodies fallen from heaven stretched out waiting naked and restless" are open to his physical visitation. As he buries his
face "in their shoulders and breasts, breathing their skin . . . bodies
locked shuddering naked, hot lips and buttocks screwed into each
other," he hears the "bride cry for forgiveness" and the groom "cov-
ered with tears of passion and compassion." What is described so sen-
sually is an orgasm of community—a nude coming together of primal
human hearts from which the poet rises "up from the bed replenished
with last intimate gestures and kisses of farewell" (*CP*, 115).

The graphic extremity to which the erotic description takes one is
an all-out blitzkrieg against shame. The bed is a possible world of

contracted time and space—the identical bed threatened by the "busy old fool, unruly Sunne" that John Donne so beautifully has celebrated in "The Sunne Rising." In Ginsberg's poem, however, it is not the "sunne" that is the intruding landlady of this secret tryst but the mind. Once again, the "cold touch of philosophy" withers primordial love. The conclusion of Ginsberg's poem drops an ironic veil between love and life as it is lived. Shameless physical love occurs

> All before the mind awakes, behind shades and closed doors in a darkened house
> where inhabitants roam unsatisfied in the night, nude ghosts seeking each other out in silence.
>
> (*CO*, 115)

Some of the pathos of Ginsberg's personal attempts to revive "nude ghosts" can be appreciated in his mock-heroic epic "The Green Automobile," a metaphorical excursion to Denver, where he imagines that he and Neal Cassady will ride in the green automobile of imagination and

> . . . be the angels of the world's desire
> and take the world to bed with us before we die.
>
> Sleeping alone, or with companion,
>   girl or fairy sheep or dream,
>   I'll fail of lacklove, you, satiety:
>   all men fall, our fathers fell before. . . .
>
> (*CP*, 86)

The poem combines Kerouac's legacy of slangy imagery, but its un-characteristically disciplined form, thirty-four staggered four-line stanzas, is pure Williams. Even with the formality of rigid stanzas, "The Green Automobile" marks a new rhetorical freedom in Gins-berg, an escape from self-consciousness, which is echoed in its theme. Love is the prize, the holy grail, of these two deprived wanderers, and the urgent necessity of drinking from this universal cup erases hetero-homosexual boundaries. *"Malest Cornifici Tuo Catullo"* is another, franker acknowledgment of homosexuality in which Ginsberg poignantly begs for Kerouac's approval of his new liaison, presumably with Peter Orlovsky:

> Ah don't think I'm sickening.
> You're angry at me. For all my lovers?
> It's hard to eat shit, without having visions;
> when they have eyes for me it's like Heaven.
>
> (*CP*, 123)

The *Ubi Sunt*

One of the universals of poetic expression is the mood of remembrance of things past. The modern *ubi sunt* sometimes arouses a poignancy that rivals even the most powerful of the Old English lyrics. The subject is the same: alienation; the mood, however, is more personal because the bygone times are less distant and the feelings register a sense of how rapidly the ravages of time close in. "The Wanderer" and "The Seafarer" give a taste of the loneliness of the unaccommodated scop, bereft of his mead hall and the comfort of his protecting thane. Modern mead halls lack the magnificence of Heorot; "matter is water" (*CP*, 201), the twentieth-century singer confesses. The heavy nostalgia of an Anglo-Saxon heritage is translated into faster tempos and tawdrier, less localized scenes. The universal feeling has not changed, but the props are demythologized. The result is a poem such as " 'Back on Time Square Dreaming of Times Square' " (*CP*, 188).

The conflict of the latter poem is measured by the collision of actuality with memory. The medium is place—Times Square—and the kinetic throwoff of the poem is the sad contrast of what is with what was. Times Square, a "memorial of ten years," is now emotionally neutralized by the imposing facticity of "the green & grooking Mc-Graw/Hill offices" (*CP*, 188). A "sad trumpeter" is petitioned to "stand on the empty streets at dawn / and blow a silver chorus to the buildings of Times Square"; but the time for silver choruses is long past—ten years—what music now exists belongs to a solitary cop walking by "invisible with his music."

Surprisingly, the contrast is not the traditional one, that is, present loneliness versus past joy. The contrast is between two distinct types of loneliness that superimposes one quality of alienation with a deeper tint of the same. The polar symbols are the McGraw-Hill offices of the present moment and the "Globe Hotel" of memory. Both poles share a grimness that the fine discrimination of the poet separates with subtle reminiscence. "I was lonely," he confesses, just as he implicitly avows his present loneliness. The modern mead hall (the "Globe Hotel") boasted little of the comfort and solace of its historical antecedents, for it was a place where

> Garver lay in gray
> gray beds there and hunched his
> back and cleaned his needles—
> where I lay many nights on the nod
> from his leftover bloody cottons
> and dreamed of Blake's voice talking. . . .
>
> (*CP*, 188)

Returning to this place is acknowledging the quickened pace of mutability:

> Garver's dead in Mexico two years, hotel's vanished into a parking lot
> And I'm back here—sitting on the streets
> again.

The *ubi sunt* lament that speaks through this poem is the forlorn query: Where are the not-so-good old days before mass media destroyed humanity's authenticity? It is a lament to the co-opted Beat Generation—a group that was popularized to extinction:

> The movies took our language, the
> great red signs
> A DOUBLE BILL OF GASSERS
> Teen Age Nightmare
> Hooligans of the Moon.
>
> (*CP*, 188)

Underlying the lament is the apologetic protest of misrepresentation:

> But we were never nightmare
> hooligans but seekers of
> the blond nose for Truth.

The theme, then, of this poem is missionary martyrdom. From the ashes of an apparently defeated memory arises the poet's conviction about the prophetic validity of what had once occurred. "We are legend," he concedes, "invisible but legendary, as prophecied" (*CP*, 188).

"My Sad Self" is a less protestant and a less prophetic poem. It is difficult to defend much of it against the charge of "crude sentimentality" that the *Times Literary Supplement* insists "is of a piece with the equally crude rhetoric, the hamfisted philosophizing, and the wholesale misuse of imagist and neosurrealist techniques" that pervade *Reality Sandwiches*. It is sentimental, but it is somewhat less so than "Tears," which is indeed an example of Ginsberg's apparent "belief that an emotion stated is an emotion conveyed."[15] "My Sad Self" baldly states an emotion—sadness—that is presented more or less as a premise as the poet gazes at New York from the top of the RCA Building. From this vantage point he catalogues various places, each with its attendant nostalgia ("my history summed up, my absences / and ecstasies in Harlem"). The universalizing lever in this poem—the device that lifts it from pure nostalgic sentimentality—is the concept of transiency that is suggested in the final lines of the first stanza:

> —sun shining down on all I own
> in one eyeblink to the horizon
> in my last eternity—
> matter is water.
> (*CP*, 201)

Ginsberg owns all he sees because of his subjective relation to it ("Who digs Los Angeles is Los Angeles!" [*CP*, 134]). The natural corollary to this stance is the intransigence of things: "matter is water."

The remainder of "My Sad Self" is a meandering journey through New York with the usual Ginsbergian reactions to what he sees about him. For example, he stares

> into all man's
> plateglass, faces,
> questioning after who loves. . . .
> (*CP*, 201)

Near the end of the poem, he unleashes his prophetic voice and painfully observes that

> this graveyard . . . once seen
> never regained or desired
> in the mind to come . . . must disappear."
> (*CP*, 202)

Norman MacCaig, who has admitted that "there's a great head of pressure built up in all that Allen Ginsberg writes," remarks that "the trouble is that often the fabric of the poem can't contain it—it explodes messily in your face, splattering you with gobbets and fragments of what may have been a fine body of experience."[16] This description seems accurate for

"FFFFF	U		U	NN			N		
F	U		U	N	N		N		
FFFFF	U		U	N	N	N		
F		U	U	N		N	N	NY DEATH."
F		U	U	N		NN		
F		UU		N		N		

"I Beg You Come Back & Be Cheerful," "Aether," and several others are similarly fragmented. In these poems, "syntax is shot at sight, things are described in a catalogue of gasps, the light is lurid, distances enormous [and] . . . the wind blows from hysteria."[17] "Aether," though, contains a justification for these excursions:

> Yet the experiments must continue!
> Every possible combination of Being—all
> the old ones! all the old Hindu
> Sabahadabadie-pluralic universes
> ringing in Grandiloquent
> Bearded
> Juxtaposition. . . .
>
> (*CP*, 242)

Many of these experiments were accomplished under the influence of various stimulants and drugs, but the literary significance is clear: the method is spontaneous dictation of experience without benefit of afterthought. Perhaps the typical reaction is, again, MacCaig's, whose summary is: "Terribly Romantic, in a diabolical sort of way. And tediously self-regarding. . . . It's the continuous pumping-up that I distrust."[18]

"Siesta in Xbalba," the best poem of *Reality Sandwiches*, is not "pumped up" at all; but, as James Scully feels, it "recalls . . . the quieter vision of Henry Vaughan."[19] What is reminiscent of Vaughan more than anything else is control. Readers are not asked to fill their minds with abstract eternities or chaotic meanderings of a turgid mind; instead, they finally have something tangible to deal with.

Ginsberg evokes a real, vibrant world that is at the same time preg-
nant with intimations of immortality.

Like Vaughan's "The World" ("I saw Eternity last night . . ."),
"Siesta in Xbalba" makes the effort for revelation:

> Late sun opening the book,
>   blank page like light,
>   invisible words unscrawled,
>   impossible syntax
> of apocalypse—.
>   (*CP*, 97)

The poem even programs a method: "let the mind fall down." From
the very beginning, therefore, the poem expresses a yearning for apocalyptic vision—which almost assures the proper mystic mood—and
promotes a yielding up of the rational discipline so that the poet may
become almost pure receptor. What occurs from this point on is what
George Poulet describes as the "infinite receptivity" that is the genius
of Walt Whitman's thought.[20] Ginsberg obviously enjoys the stance.
He is in a hammock, suspended, so to speak, above the world and
yet still of it, while white doves copulate underneath him and mon-
keys bark (*CP*, 97). We learn that the poet has "succumbed to this
temptation" of "doing nothing but lying in a hammock" and that he
is prepared for observation and apocalyptic musing.

The musing initially takes place in the form of a dream flashback—
"an eternal kodachrome," Ginsberg calls it—where his friends at a
party are frozen in his mind. Clearly, the idea is to present an inauthentic contrast to the authentic situation the poet is in because the
people at the party are described as "posed together," with "stylized
gestures" and "familiar visages." They are all

> posturing in one frame,
> superficially gay
> or tragic as may be,
> illumed with the fatal
> character and intelligent
> actions of their lives.
>   (*CP*, 98)

Immediately following this dream flashback is a description of the
poet's own pretentiously stark surroundings:

And I in a concrete room
above the abandoned
labyrinth of Palenque
measuring my fate,
wandering solitary in the wild
—blinking singleminded
at a bleak idea—.

(*CP*, 98)

Clearly, there is a note of superiority here. Friends are trivial but "I" am serious is the note Ginsberg seems to strike; but the usual cosmic trump card remains to be played: the oncoming mystic vision. Fatigued from gazing at the bleak idea, the poet awaits the moment when

my soul might shatter
at one primal moment's
sensation of the vast
movement of divinity.

(*CP*, 98–99)

There is an inchoate quest operating in the debris of mind that has fallen down, and it seems to be directed toward the eternity that is so often the misty goal in Ginsberg's poems. The reason is probably the same as Whitman's: "Eternity gives similitude to all periods and locations and processes, and animates and inanimates forms, and . . . is the bond of time."[21] Such a valuable force as this bond is certainly worthy of the highest poetry, and it helps once again to explain Ginsberg's views concerning drugs. If eternity is the "bond of time"—the element that glues everything together into community and permits everyone to be an angel—then it is reasonable that any access to this state is well worth the price. Even without drugs the search for eternity can be salutary:

As I leaned against a tree
inside the forest
expiring of self-begotten love,
I looked up at the stars absently,
as if looking for
something else in the blue night

> through the boughs,
> and for a moment saw myself
> leaning against a tree. . . .
>   (*CP*, 99)

Time and eternity, as the glue that binds everything together, is developed as a concept later in the poem when Ginsberg meditates upon a "death's-head." Part of his fascination lies in its relevance to the principle of prophecy. He is impressed by the fact that it

> thinks its way
> through centuries the thought of the same night in which I sit
> in skully meditation.
>   (*CP*, 101).

Here is an instance of eternity indeed obliterating time but in the fashion of biblical prophecy. The anterior artisan, the maker of the head, sculpted his artifact until it fully represented his idea; but now, Ginsberg muses, the death's-head communicates that idea across time:

> but now his fine thought's vaguer
> than my dream of him:
> and only the crude skull figurement's
> gaunt insensible glare is left. . . .
>   (*CP*, 101)

The philosophical substratum of this small passage of the poem seems to be the idea that truth (even history) is entirely subjective. Works of art, be they poems about death's-heads, have the capability of triggering or exciting thoughts in future individuals. The sense of oneness that eternity brings with it acts as a sort of guarantee of this phenomenon and presents the possibility of bridges across time. Real history, then, does not operate chronologically, logically, or rationally. History is apocalypse, so that Ginsberg can say:

> I alone know the great crystal door
>   to the House of Night
> a legend of centuries
>   —I and a few Indians.
>   (*CP*, 103)

Any other access to the history—any other solution to the "impossible syntax" of the hieroglyphics—cannot possibly yield what the death's-head can surrender subjectively to the eternalized viewer. Unless the mind is allowed to "fall down," the rational apparatus will filter out the past:

> Time's slow wall overtopping
>   all that firmament of mind,
> as if a shining waterfall of leaves and rain
> were built down solid from the endless sky
> through which no thought can pass.
>   (*CP*, 102)

The first part of the poem ends with a rejection and a tentative affirmation: "There is a god / dying in / America" (*CP*, 105), which is the institutionalized religious impulse. At the same time, there is also

> an inner
> anterior image
> of divinity
> beckoning me out
> to pilgrimage.
>   (*CP*, 106)

Part two of this poem, "Return to the United States," possesses a stark, generally crisp, descriptive style and only one real intrusion of Ginsbergian metaphysics. The reader is told, finally, that "the problem is isolation" (*CP*, 108), a statement followed later by the lament: "What solitude I've finally inherited" (*CP*, 109). These lines appear to mean that Ginsberg has failed in a way. If what he hoped to retain from his night in Xbalba was a vision of Whitman's

> vast similitude [that] interlocks all,
> All spheres grown, ingrown, small, large, suns, moons, planets,
> All distances of place however wide,
> all distances of time, . . .[22]

what he actually returned with was less ambitious:

        a few Traditions,
        metrical, mystical, manly
        . . . and certain characteristic flaws.
                                        (*CP*, 110)

But the isolation, it would seem, is not entirely his own; it is the isolation of the whole universe. The temptation of social criticism becomes too strong in the final lines, and the real loneliness and the real isolation are finally diagnosed as natural consequences of "The nation over the border [America]" that "grinds its arms and dreams of war" (*CP*, 110).

Intellectual sentimentality seems to be Ginsberg's Achilles heel, and one reason for the success of "Siesta in Xbalba" is the fact that the thundering onslaughts upon God, eternity, the cosmos, and so on, are kept unusually under control. There is more attention to real objects in this poem than in most of the others, which anchors it to a refreshing empirical plane too often missing in the later work. An oriental clarity in some places even brings metaphysics nearer to the reader's grasp, much in the way suggested in "Cézanne's Ports," for example. One such instance is the simple description of the night in the midst of the rain forest:

                    I can see the moon
        moving over the edge of the night forest
                and follow its destination
        through the clear dimensions of the sky
                    from end to end of the dark
        circular horizon.
                                        (*CP*, 100)

If nothing else, the idea in this short excerpt is rendered rather than garrulously bellowed. It is structural, not strident, and the quiet control of "Siesta in Xbalba" is a welcome reminder that the best poems are most often made rather than notated.

Assessment

It is very difficult to assess *Reality Sandwiches* as a whole because the book, which spans seven years of poetic development, modestly claims to be merely "scribbed secret notebooks, and wild typewritten pages, for yr own joy" (*CP*, 801). It would be silly to pretend that many of the poems are not simply amateurish, pretentious, clumsy, and, at times, downright dull. One bittersweet review concedes that "in among this amateurish material . . . there are moments of real excitement, and poems which are firmly restrained and delicately balanced. There are not many, but there are enough to give one hope for Mr. Ginsberg's future development."[23] The assessment is probably true, but what the reviewer hopefully regards as signs of "future development" are perhaps more accurately carry-overs from Ginsberg's less flamboyant earlier versifying. Ginsberg is not working toward what would be considered traditional control; he is fleeing from it as rapidly as possible.

One is left, then, with the kind of response to which James Scully invariably resorts when he reviews Ginsberg's work; Scully finds Ginsberg's worth in his "sense of humanity." The phrase is ambiguous and slippery, and even Scully's attempt to clarify does no more than suggest the type of power he finds in the poems. Nevertheless, according to Scully this sense of humanity is Ginsberg's attempt "to uncover a community";[24] and such attempts have perfectly respectable credentials. Walt Whitman, for example, was doing the very same thing when he wrote:

Divine am I inside and out, and I make holy whatever I touch or am touched from,
The scent of these arm-pits aroma finer than prayer,
This head more than churches, bibles, and all creeds.[25]

In a way, Whitman's liturgy of the divine, human self appears to be the one constant, yet elusive, goal toward which Ginsberg consistently strives. One form of its progress appears in "Sather Gate Illumination," where the final lines declare that "Who loves himself loves me who love myself" (*CP,* 145), but the fullest expression comes in "The Change" (*CP,* 324) and those poems that follow it.

Chapter Seven
Planet News and *The Fall of America*

Planet News

Planet News collects the poems that Ginsberg wrote from 1961 to 1967 and is particularly interesting because it covers work completed both before and after that moment on the Kyoto-Tokyo Express when he awoke to realize: "My energies of the last . . . oh, 1948 to 1963, all completely washed up." He had completed a cycle and was aware that "to attain the depth of consciousness that I was seeking . . . I had to cut myself off from the Blake vision and renounce it."

Renouncing Blake meant giving up a commitment to a memory of an experience and taking on instead "the total awareness of now." It was as if Blake's voice were suddenly transformed into Williams's and the new command was to seek "cosmic consciousness" not in visions but in "contact with what was going on around me." "In order to get back to now . . . or direct vision of the moment, . . . I'd have to give up this continual churning thought process of yearning back to a visionary state."[1]

The public mission of this volume is to give news of the planet, but, as Helen Vendler points out, there is considerable private news as well.[2] "This Form of Life Needs Sex," for instance, informs us with "fermenting specificity" of Ginsberg's homosexuality and its frustrating awareness that "Between me and oblivion an unknown woman stands; / Not the Muse but living meat-phantom, a mystery scary as my fanged god . . . " (*CP*, 284). A private resolution to change the direction of his life prompts "Last Night in Calcutta," in which a sick and disconsolate Ginsberg vows to

> —Leave immortality for another to suffer like a fool,
> not get stuck in the corner of the universe
> sticking morphine in the arm and eating meat.
>
> (*CP*, 301)

There are travel poems—"Elan perceptions notated at Mediterranean, Galilee & Ganges" (*CP*, 815)—and poems reflecting "tenement doldrums" (*CP*, 815), but the poems baring the "public" news of the planet, for all their sometimes comic zest, are as grimly cynical as this assessment Ginsberg made in 1969: "this planet is in the midst of a probably fatal sickness; the by-products of that sickness include not only the political violence of real-estate developers but all the giant fantasies of the Cold War—the witch-hunts, race paranoia, projections of threat and doom. The sickness will end in our destroying our own planet."[3]

The first public news is "Television Was a Baby Crawling toward That Deathchamber" (*CP*, 272–83), a surreal, eighteen-page outpouring of apparent imaginative chaos, which Ginsberg describes thematically as "electronic politics disassociation & messianic rhapsody" (*CP*, 815) and poetically as "full chaotic consciousness."[4] Paul Zweig found it "the quintessential poem of 'too much,' " meaning by "too much" a Whitmanesque inclusiveness that in Ginsberg "opens a hot line to every recess of his roomy, endless body." The poem is structured with the characteristic long-line breath unit, which makes it a kind of elastic container like *Howl* that, Zweig remarks, "works against the very idea of poetic form" but at the same time "claims for itself all the privileges of form, i.e., the privilege of being this irreplaceable, absolutely achieved word-vision."[5]

Unlike *Howl*, "Television Was a Baby" has a much looser, diffuse energy, a diluted rage whose exaggerations as often as not end in comedy. Its theme (Moloch, the institutional enemy of human goodness) parallels that of *Howl*, the poem once again cataloguing the dehumanizing efforts of "billionaire" media manipulators, "State legislatures filled with Capital Punishment Fiends," and "vast Custom agencies searching books" (*CP*, 277) who prey on "the Saintly Meat of the Heart . . . our feelings!" (*CP*, 274). The deliberate comic energy that moves just underneath the outrage of *Howl* is in this poem too, but because the outrage here is so unfocused, the hyperbolic comedy seems to steal the show.

For all its apocalyptic fulmination against the Moloch-minded forces at work in America, Ginsberg has fun with this poem; the uncontrolled image-juxtapositioning is pure zany indulgence—the wilder and more outrageous the better:

Six Billionaires that own all Time since the Gnostic Revolt in Aegypto—

they built the Sphinx to confuse my sex life, Who Fucked the Void?

(CP, 280)

And yet, the seriousness of the theme does break through, and in the same unruly form:

Six thousand movietheatres, 100,000,000 television sets, a billion radios, wires and wireless crisscrossing hemispheres, semaphore lights and morse, all telephones ringing at once connect every mind by its ears to one vast consciousness This Time Apocalypse—everybody waiting for one mind to Break thru—.

(CP, 280)

Awaiting the breakthrough of "one mind" is vintage Ginsberg— vision-haunted Ginsberg before "The Change." In two years, after his "picaresque around the world globe" (CP, 815), including visits to the Holy Land and talks with Martin Buber, documented in "Galilee Shore" (CP, 289), he will have absorbed the understanding that India had to offer him: "At the time [of Howl] I believed in some sort of God and thus Angels, and religiousness—at present as Buddhist I see an awakened emptiness (Sûnyatâ) as the crucial term."[6] Perhaps we can detect an anticipation of this spiritual change in "Death News," Ginsberg's moving account of his reaction to reading William Carlos Williams's obituary in Time:

. . . now I saw Passaic
and Ganges one, consenting his devotion,
because he walked on the steely bank & prayed
to a Goddess in the river, that he only invented,
another Ganga-Ma.

(CP, 297)

The blending of the Ganges and the Passaic symbolically unites the influences of Buddhism and Williams; Ginsberg had come full circle.

Prior to his Asian trip, Ginsberg had, as he put it, painted himself into a corner with drugs. Although taking drugs made him nauseous, he continued to take them, not, it appears, because of addiction so much as because he felt he was "duly bound and obliged for the sake of consciousness expansion . . . and seeking more direct contact with primate sensation, nature, to continue."[7] Part of the problem was an identity crisis. Drug-induced hallucinations had made him question

the validity of his own identity, not to mention his fear of being literally melted into the universe. The portion of Ginsberg's letter to
William Burroughs, mentioned before, describing his experience
with *yage* reveals the magnitude of his preoccupation with self and
death under the influence of these powerful drugs.[8] Later he describes
the subject of his hallucination as "a Being whose presence I had not
yet fully sensed."[9]

What worried Ginsberg at this point was the question of authentic
reality: which was real—his vision or his normal consciousness? Burroughs's reply to Ginsberg's appeal for consolation is interesting:
"Your AYUASKA consciousness is more valid than 'Normal Consciousness'? Whose 'Normal Consciousness'?"[10] Ginsberg was under great
pressure to continue his exploration into the nonhuman dimensions of
consciousness. His feeling was that he should not fear death but pursue it. Death was God, and to attain God, he had to leave his body—
die.

The Asian trip occasioned the reversal of this line of thought. He
found that the object of his quest was not something outside himself—the complete consciousness that Death seemed to promise—but
rather his own heart within. The implications of this realization were
enormous, for it meant renouncing virtually all of his previous com-
mitments; it even meant renouncing Blake.

"The Change, Kyoto-Tokyo Express" documents this crucial turning point in Ginsberg's life. The poem itself is not remarkable, and
the reader can be very easily put off by its incessant and somewhat
precious easternisms (Ginsberg supplies notes for some of the more
exotic images, reminding one of a recently returned traveler adding
commentary to his colored slides). The message is succinct but repeti-
tive: no more visions; live in the skin and the present tense.

"Wales Visitation"

"Wales Visitation," unquestionably one of Ginsberg's most effective poems, appears near the end of *Planet News*. It was written four
years after "The Change" under the influence of LSD. The poem warrants consideration here because it realizes so many of the aims voiced
in "The Change," particularly Ginsberg's quiet liberation from visions, his induced sense of oneness with a strikingly particularized
physical world, and his awareness of breath as the instrument that effects it all. Although the theme of the meditation is strikingly similar

to the much earlier poem "Transcription of Organ Music" (*CP,* 140), it owes much to its Welsh locale and the hermetic tradition. There is a flavor of Henry Vaughan but also the imprint of Blake in its presumption that heaven is manifest in a grain of sand. Ginsberg updates these notions, of course, and bends them to his private purposes. The poem is an exorcism, for Ginsberg still suffers pressure from his demon visions, but it is also an implicit postmodernist confirmation of epistemological assumptions of the sort urged by Charles Olson's *Human Universe* that the traditional Western subject-object stance toward reality be abandoned in favor of epistemological humiliation (with humanity understood as merely one entity among others in nature).[11]

The vivid detail of the images in "Wales Visitation" is the poem's main strength and Ginsberg credits it to his renunciation of visions and subjective self-consciousness: "the most telling of the details is the line '. . . of the satanic thistle that raises its horned symmetry flowering above sister grass-daisies' pink tiny bloomlets angelic as lightbulbs—" (*CP,* 480). This is practically microscopic observation of detail: "It occurred to me that I could do this sort of thing by turning my eyes outside of my head and stop trying to reproduce my Blake visions of cosmic consciousness, which was subtly and truly there behind it all. But, on this acid trip, I finally found the path or the technique or the way to direct my attention outside of myself. . . . All I had to do was see what was in front of me!"[12]

Freedom for objectivity was gained partially through exorcising the old visions. "Any time I felt a sense of mental unbalance or destabiliziation or that 'cosmic, demonic terror,' I would just sit there on the hillside," Ginsberg tells us. "But, I was still projecting my breath onto the cosmos, comparing the heavens and the air and the atmosphere over England and over the valley to an ocean tide slowly moving. Then I compared that same breath that came out of my body with the air that soughed through trees."[13]

The functional importance of the breath in this experience demonstrates Ginsberg's sympathy with Olson's "projective" poetics and the "stance toward reality" it presupposes. Breath, as Olson meant it (and as Ginsberg appears to mean, liberates the self from the mind and places it physically in the body so that our knowing of the world, our experience and discovery, comes from "inside us / & at the same time does not feel literally identical with our physical or mortal self."[14] Ginsberg acknowledges this power of breath even to regretting later his creative dependence in "Wales Visitation" on LSD: "Well, paying attention to the breath wipes out that self-consciousness. I would say meditation is above acid, ultimately. I must admit it. I was wrong all along."[15] What he had gained through "Wales Visitation" was a "realization that me making noise as poetry was no different from the wind making noise in the branches. It was just as natural. It was a *very important point*. The fact that there were thoughts flowing through the mind is as much of a natural object as is the milky way floating over the Isle of Skye."[16]

Of course, Ginsberg arrives at this position from an Eastern approach and with the biochemical assistance of LSD, but the result is the same:

> the great secret is no secret
> > Senses fit the winds,
> > > Visible is visible,
> > rain-mist curtains wave through the bearded vale,
> > > gray atoms wet the wind's kabbala
> Crosslegged on a rock in dusk rain,
> > rubber booted in soft grass, mind moveless,
> breath trembles in white daisies by the roadside,
> > > Heaven breath and my own symmetric
> Airs wavering thru antlered green fern
> drawn in my navel, same breath as breathes thru Capel-Y-Ffn,
> > Sounds of Aleph and Aum
> > > through forests of gristle,
> > my skull and Lord Hereford's Knob equal,
> > > > All Albion one.
>
> > > > > (*CP,* 482)

Several smaller poems in *Planet News* testify to Ginsberg's erratic but abiding allegiance to Williams's objectivism. "Portland Coliseum" and "First Party at Ken Kesey's with Hell's Angels" both pattern themselves after Williams's technique of structurally rendering meaningful ironies through sheer arrangement of meticulous, detailed images. In both poems, a scene capturing the essence of countercultural exuberance (a rock concert and a party), which makes up the bulk of piece, is then threateningly framed by an image of authoritarian menace. "Portland Coliseum," for example, ends with this contentious stanza:

> > . . . a line of police with
> > > folded arms stands
> > Sentry to contain the red

                                          sweatered ecstasy
                                   that rises upward to the
                                            wired roof.
                                                                (CP, 366)

Similarly, in "First Party at Ken Kesey's,"

> . . . the huge wooden house, a yellow chandelier
> at 3AM the blast of loudspeakers
> hi-fi Rolling Stones Ray Charles Beatles
> Jumping Joe Jackson and twenty youths
> dancing to the vibration thru the floor,

and even "children sleeping softly in their bedroom bunks," all un-
leash their dionysian, libertarian joy to a stolid audience of "4 police
cars parked outside the painted / gate, red lights revolving in the
leaves" (CP, 374). These poems are accessible to ordinary readers of
poetry, are fine candidates for general poetry anthologies,[17] and are
pure Williams in their rendering.

Kral Majales

The other poems after "The Change" seem to become more and
more political—perhaps as a consequence of the renunciation of the
visions. There is, of course, his occasional poem "Kral Majales," written in honor of his being crowned King of May in Prague and probably a partial cause of his expulsion. The long, clanky line
characterizes the form of this poem, and there is the usual frank scatology. Remnants of Indian religious mythology appear like postcards
tucked away in the bottom of old valises, but there is also a concern
for what is happening in today's social world that is somehow a pleasant relief from the former self-indulgent quests for self-knowledge.
And the new spirit of "telling it like it is" of these later poems no
doubt served to endear Ginsberg to the sixties generation.

The poem opens with criticism of Communists and capitalists,
both of whom in various ways bring intolerable pressures upon "the
Just man" (CP, 353). The logic of the attack becomes a bit clearer
when it is explained later in the poem that Ginsberg was "arrested
thrice in Prague." The series of indignities that occur to him in the
course of these arrests are documented, but are finally atoned for when

he is crowned the King of May. *Kral Majales* soon takes on a symbolic significance; it represents "the power of sexual youth," "Industry in eloquence," "action in amour," and "old Human poesy." Ginsberg has been chosen King of May because he "heard the voice of Blake in a vision, / and repeat[s] that voice," because he "sleeps with teenagers laughing," because he "may be expelled from my Kingdom with honor, as of old, / To show the differences between Caesar's Kingdom and the Kingdom of the May of Man." The last reason seems to be the most comprehensive; it embraces the usual we-feel-and-love-one-another versus you-calculate-and-brutalize-humanity attitude of hipdom.

The rest of the poem is a rather eclectic catalogue of sights, sounds, and random thoughts that occur to Ginsberg en route to London. There seems to be no particular pattern to the observations; many, in fact, seem mawkishly sentimental.

The Fall of America

When Ginsberg cited *Wichita Vortex Sutra* as the "keystone section of a progressively longer poem on 'These States'," (*CP*, 815), one wonders if he did not have in mind by the term *longer poem* a project akin to such earlier indigenous efforts as the *Columbiad, Song of Myself, The Bridge, Paterson*, and *The Maximus Poems* in the quest for what Roy Harvey Pearce once called "the American equivalent of the epic."[18] All of these vast enterprises were in one sense geographical, seeking to discover the essential integrity of the American New World through the concept of place, and in reading Ginsberg's "Poem of These States" (*CP*, 369), which is a "chronicle taperecorded scribed by hand or sung condensed, the flux of car bus airplane dream consciousness" (*CP*, 815), one agrees with Helen Vendler that in *The Fall of America*, at least, "Ginsberg has become a geographer, and his one inexhaustible subject is the earth and what it looks like."[19]

We do witness a poetic mapping of America in these poems, but it may be the case for some readers that, as Ginsberg himself was fond of repeating (borrowing from Korzybski and General Semantics), the map is not the territory. If not the territory, then what? In Chapter Two we savored Ginsberg's musing remark in the *Indian Journals*: "how do you write poetry about poetry (not as objective abstract subject matter à la Robert Duncan or Pound)—but making use of a radical method of eliminating subject matter altogether. . . . I seem to be delaying a step forward in this field (elimination of subject matter) and hanging on to habitual humanistic series of autobiographical photographs . . . although my own Consciousness has gone beyond the conceptual to non-conceptual episodes of experience inexpressible by old means of humanistic storytelling."[20] These poems, while indeed offering an "avalanche of detail"[21] of and about America, are "non-conceptual episodes of experience," which Ginsberg elsewhere has described as "the sequence of thought-forms passing naturally through ordinary mind" (*CP,* xx). Ginsberg usually frames this notion with the slogans "First thought, best thought," and "Mind is shapely, Art is shapely"—injunctions that appear to legitimize the process of spontaneous writing, that is, the mere registry of free-flow consciousness.

That conciousness is, of course, Ginsberg's and if we find it "shapely," then the art that emerges from it must, in principle, be "shapely" too. Williams's "Dr. Paterson" and Olson's "Maximus" were epic personae whose shapely visions unified the details of Paterson and Gloucester, fashioning from the multiplicity of raw detail an objective, conceptual unity—a shapeliness—that was achieved through conscious craft. But Ginsberg, perhaps like Pound in *The Cantos,* surrenders on principle to his admittedly eccentric ego for whatever integrity we find in *The Fall of America,* as well as in its complements *Wichita Vortex Sutra* and *Iron Horse.*[22] Perhaps as a consequence it draws comments from critics unsympathetic to that ego about "the silliness and bum writing that is to be found in much of *The Fall of America.*"[23]

The geography that Ginsberg maps in these poems is not really the United States of America, but the anarchic commonwealth of Ginsberg's consciousness, which, through his characteristic mode of juxtaposing images, is recorded on all its levels simultaneously.

Wichita Vortex Sutra

As Ginsberg apocalyptically describes it, *Wichita Vortex Sutra* (the "keystone section" of "These States") presents "Self sitting in its own meat throne" invoking "Harekrishna as preserver of human planet," challenging "all other Powers usurping State Consciousness to recognize same Identity, and thus delivering the sacred formula bringing peace:

> I lift my voice aloud,
>> make Mantra of American language now,

> pronounce the words beginning my own millennium,
> 'I here declare the End of the War!' "
>
> (*CP*, 815).

Paul Carroll assumes that "Ginsberg attempts to make a mantra out of the American language itself," claiming that the poem is "embodying an experience of contemporary American language and what that language can or cannot accomplish."[24] This focus on the cultural irresponsibility of language reveals the thematic kinship of *Wichita Vortex Sutra* to Williams's *Paterson* and Charles Olson's *Maximus Poems*, all three works lamenting a pathological separation of language from reality. Regrettably, in Carroll's estimation at least, the mantra fails in *Wichita Vortex Sutra*, for after giving countless examples of the perversion of language prior to the mantra in the poem, Ginsberg shows us no improvement after the mantra: "Not only is the language undistinguished and prosy but in several crucial instances the diction disintegrates into bad or flashy rhetoric."[25]

A long piece (fifteen pages in its original pamphlet), *Wichita Vortex Sutra* recalls Dante with its sensation of sweeping us into the vortex of some kind of American linguistic hell. If there be such a thing as "anti-poetic," this poem might qualify on the grounds that it spills over into television commercials, newspaper headlines, radio diskjockey patter, news broadcasts, neon signs—in short, all the semantic flotsam and jetsam that has inundated American life.

There are several subjects in the poem. The Vietnam war appears on the surface to be the overriding concern, but as the reader is swept closer and closer to the vortex of consternation, it soon becomes apparent that war is merely a symptom of something even more basic: the elemental violence of humanity. Most calamitous events have their beginnings in trivia, and Ginsberg finds the genesis of American violence (the vortex) not only in Wichita (midcenter U.S.A.) but in a particular building in Wichita: the Hotel Eaton. The reason?

> Carrie Nation began the war on Vietnam here
> with an angry smashing axe
> attacking Wine—
> Here fifty years ago, by her violence
> began a vortex of hatred that defoliated the Mekong Delta.
>
> (*CP*, 410)

One message of the poem, then, is the contagion of violence that has spread across America and has even been exported overseas.

A second message is about language. As Ginsberg conceives language in this poem, it is magic power. It can provide "Black Magic language, formulas for reality" (*CP*, 401), or it can reflect the sameness of all human hearts, at which time it merits the name *prophecy*. Prophecy is equivalent to truth; "formulas for reality" are deceptions, disguised lies, "bad guesses," and all the paraphernalia that comes between what really happens and one's apprehension of it. They are unreliable maps that distort the territory they allegedly mirror. The news media are guilty of manufacturing such maps:

> Has anyone looked in the eyes of the wounded?
> Have we seen but paper faces, Life Magazine?
> Are screaming faces made of dots,
>   electric dots on Television. . . .
>
> (*CP*, 400)

Wichita Vortex Sutra, then, is really a poem about "how to speak the right language" (*CP*, 405); it is also a lament over the "Sorcerer's Apprentice who lost control / of the simplest broomstick in the world: / Language" (*CP*, 401). The apprentice is the administration who is responsible for the fact that "almost all our language has been taxed by war" (*CP*, 406). The evidence comes blaring through the car radio as Ginsberg speeds across the midwestern plains, and it screams from the front pages of the *Lincoln Star*, the *Albuquerque Journal* and "NBCBSUPAPINSLIFE." The heinousness of the situation is that "all this black language [is] writ by machine!" (*CP*, 405). The parallelism to Olson's notion of "mu-sick" in *The Maximus Poems* is unmistakable.[26]

The antidote for this sick language is a familiar prescription: prophecy. Prophecy is based upon the fact that "All we do is for this frightened thing / we call Love" and that "spoken lonesomeness is Prophecy" (*CP*, 405). The power potential for prophecy is simply that it is the most fundamental communication between humans; it assumes that the hearts of a Vietnamese and an American are the same. It acknowledges

> that the rest of the earth is unseen
>   the outer universe invisible.
>   Unknown except thru
>   language
>   airprint
>   magic images

or prophecy of the secret
                    —heart the same
              —in Waterville as Saigon one human
      form:
              When a woman's heart bursts in Waterville
              a woman screams equal in Hanoi—.
                                              (*CP*, 404)

The poem gains in intensity as it nears the climax: the arrival at Wichita. Ginsberg manages to build a structural suspense through his usual strategy of cumulative images. In this case, the cataloguing is almost entirely from communications media and commercial ideograms ("Supermarket Texaco brilliance . . . ." "ooh! sensitive city lights of Hamburger & Skelley's Gas . . . ." etc.); but the sheer energy that is released somehow makes the fantastic conclusion of the poem seem almost credible:

      Proud Wichita! vain Wichita
              cast the first stone!—
              that murdered my mother
      who died of the communist anticommunist psychosis
      in the madhouse one decade long ago. . . .
                                              (*CP*, 410)

The Fall of America won the National Book Award in 1974 by virtue of its apparently brute poetic ability to bulldoze a passionate admonishment into its sympathetic listerners' consciousness. It has, as Helen Vendler accurately points out, two subjects: "the state of America and the state of his life."[27] The reader is at pains to take the one without the other, since the premise of the enterprise as poetry seems to be their absolute inextricability. Thus, such abasing poems as "Please Master" (*CP*, 494) and "On Neal's Ashes" (*CP*, 505), as well as the many private confessional interludes in the longer pieces, sound a personal counterpoint to a larger public malaise. For many, this counterpoint is a severe liability. William Pritchard, for example, bemoans the "endless moaning about Neal Cassady, Jack, Gregory and the rest of that broken up old gang of his," and further complains that "on sex Ginsberg is maudlin and hysterical; on Vietnam and pollution at home he says all the right things but doesn't do much more than *say* them. His world is full of good guys and bad guys: Cleaver and Tim Leary hurrah; Lyndon Johnson, J. Edgar Hoover, Rush boo." Most of all, it is "the lack of complex ideas"[28] that distresses Pritchard about *The Fall of America*.

Ed Sanders argues that to absorb the new direction that Ginsberg blazes for poetry in these poems "you have to be willing to jump into the Ginsbergian brain-stream where the ride is gentle, comradely, and brilliant."[29] Those unopen to the celebration of Buddhist, homosexual, prophetic, and narcotic biases will find the ride more jarring than gentle, more threatening than comradely, and more uncrafted than brilliant, and they might also agree with Karl Shapiro that when poets feel that they are experiencing history or the universe, you may be sure they are about to make fools of themselves.[30]

Iron Horse

Much of what has been said of *Wichita Vortex Sutra* and *The Fall of America* applies to the separately published *Iron Horse*. This is another vast montage of taped and scribbled thoughts, feelings, and observations occurring during a train and bus journey across America during the turbulent sixties. It is no travelogue; what the reader experiences in the poem is not reality, unless, to use Ginsberg's words, "you want to define reality as *what we see*." He hastens to add, "But, we *can* know what we see. We can't know reality, but we can know what we see. So that makes it easy: all you have to do is report what you see directly, or hear directly. That makes it like rolling off a log. You don't have to delve and analyze for reality. All you have to do is be aware of what you just saw."[31]

Such "log rolling" takes place on the boundaries separating honest art from self-indulgence, and the poem's opening of self-abasement and masturbation in the roomette of a transcontinental train ("Oh what a wretch I am! What / monster naked in this metal box" [*CP*, 433 1]) recalls Marianne Moore's perhaps fastidious objection to being poetically taken with Ginsberg to the toilet: "Do I have to? I do if you take me with you in your book."[32] In the face of the "Fall of America" that *Iron Horse* prophesies, fastidiousness is perhaps an irrelevance, and even the private intimacies that the poet forces on us might be justified in terms of contributing to the accumulative "vision" of sixties America that results.

Iron Horse is, after all, Ginsberg's American mosaic, his selection of representative detail, and so we must heed his warning: "—my voice an overdramatic madman's / murmuring to myself late afternoon drowze—" (*CP*, 434). The poem's integrity is supplied by the salutary Buddhist attitude it eventually strikes. After a mélange of ironic scraps of overheard dialogue—

> "Where've they learnt the lesson? Grammarschool
> taught 'em Newspaper language.
> D'they buy it at Safeway with Reader's Digest?"
>   (*CP*, 455)

(speech that illustrates how language itself has become medium of bad Karma)—*Iron Horse* begins a catalogue of its menace:

>   The Karma
>   accumulated bombing Vietnam
>   The Karma bodies napalm-burned
>   Karma suspicion . . .
>   The Karma of bullets in the back of the head . . .
>   The Karma of babies . . . bawling destroyed
>   The Karma of populations moved from from center to center of
>   Detention
>   Karma of bribery, Karma blood-money.
>   (*CP*, 452)

"Such karmic patterns," we are instructed by the notes, "may be altered and their energy made wholesome through meditative mindfulness, conscious awareness, the practice of appreciation, which burns up karma on the spot" (*CP*, 782), and thus:

> Only a miracle appearing in Man's eyes
>   only boys' flesh singing
>   can show the warless way—.
>   (*CP*, 452)

Angkor Wat

Because *Angkor Wat* was published separately in 1968 by the Fulcrum Press with impressive accompanying photographs by Alexandra Lawrence, readers could be so struck by the pictorial magnificence of the enterprise that they might assume the poem, like the illustrations, addresses a place. It does, of course, register Angkor Wat as physical place, but place primarily as the occasion for heavy internal brooding, Ginsberg rationalizes that the poem

"At least moves from perception to obsession
according to waves of Me-ness
Still clinging to the Earthen straw
My eye."

(*CP*, 315)

This seems a true assessment. The "obsessions" are manifestly familiar; Ginsberg experiences "strokes of fear" over his body ("cancer
Bubonic / heart failure / bitter stomach juices / a wart growing on
my rib" [*CP*, 306]); his diet ("I'm not going to eat meat anymore"
[*CP*, 309]); his courage ("I'm just an old Uncle Tom in disguise all
along / afraid of physical tanks" [*CP*, 310]); drugs ("Home to the
Needle, further violation / or is this vegetable smoke and vein
warmth futile . . ." [*CP*, 313]); his sexuality (". . . why do I not
even faintly desire those / black silk girls in the alley . . ." [*CP*,
313]); religious conviction ("Nothing but a false Buddha afraid
of / my own annihilation" [*CP*, 310]); and even his literary compe-
tence ("Just a lot of words and propaganda / I been spreading getting
scared / of my own bullshit . . ." [*CP*, 315]). Everywhere it's the fear
I got in my own / intestines" (*CP*, 318), he confesses. "I am Coward
in every direction" (*CP*, 313).

The poem chronicles a dark, transitional time in Ginsberg's life; it
was written just a little over one month before "The Change." He
had just experienced a falling out with Peter Orlovsky, who had told
him that he was "washed up," had "sold out to go teach in Vancou-
ver," and had "broken [a] poetry vow."[33] It was indeed time for a
change, and Ginsberg was just beginning to feel a shift in his life
orientation that would release him from his visions and return him to
the body and the physical world—a shift anticipated in the closing
lines of "Last Night in Calcutta":

—Leave immortality for another to suffer like a fool,
not get stuck in the corner of the universe
sticking morphine in the arm and eating meat.

(*CP*, 302)

Much of *Angkor Wat*'s power, particularly in its opening passages,
emerges from the same meditative matrix as "Wales Visitation." An
almost hermetic correspondence between the poet and the physical
place about him is effected through such pathetic fallacies as

"paranoia / Banyans," "high muscled tree" with "long snaky toes spread down" (*CP*, 306), and even one tree that "needed a haircut" (*CP*, 308). Exterior landscape transposes to interior terrain, which reveals itself in montage. Like a bird building its nest of discarded fragments, Ginsberg builds an image of a militarized and journalized Southeast Asia of scraps of dialogue " 'I am inert' . . . 'I'm just doing my / Professional duty' . . . 'I'm scheming / murders' . . . 'I'm chasing a story' " (*CP*, 309). Framed against the chaos of a disintegrating ancient civilization are Ginsberg's personal efforts toward spiritual buttressing: "Buddha save me . . ." (*CP*, 314).

Angkor Wat is a tumultuous, often moving prolegomenon to "The Change," which crystallizes so much of the anxious despair and self-doubt of the earlier poem into a new and apparently lasting commitment.

Chapter Eight
Mind Breaths and *Plutonian Ode*

Mind Breaths

The back cover for *Mind Breaths* describes a potpourri of formal ingredients: "Australian songsticks . . . broken-leg meditations . . . quiet Sung sunlit greybeard soliloquies, English moonlit night-gleams, ambitious mid-life fantasies," but the most formally significant item in the list in terms of Ginsberg's meditative development is "cross-legged thoughts sitting straight-spine paying attention to empty breath flowing round the globe" (*CP*, 816). It is from this meditative posture that the volume gains it name.

We should be cautious about making any overt connections between meditative technique and poetic form; Ginsberg insists that "poetic practice is sort of like an independent carpentry that goes on by itself,"[1] but when an author's poems "compose an autobiography" (*CP*, xix) whose motif is "the sequence of thought-forms passing naturally through ordinary mind" (*CP*, xx), it is hard to ignore a correspondence. Ginsberg himself concedes that "the meditation experience . . . made me more and more aware of the humor of the fact that breath is the basis of poetry and song—it's so important in it as a measure."[2]

The specific form of Tibetan meditation that Ginsberg eventually learned from Tibetan Lama Chögyam Trungpa in 1973 at the Naropa seminary in Wyoming was the "simple *samatha*." As Ginsberg explains it, *samatha* is a Sanskrit word that means "pacification . . . tranquilization of mind style," although Trungpa often defined it as a "wakefulness or mindfulness" that made thought "more and more transparent and less and less obsessive," leading to an "insight . . . or awareness of detail" called *vipasyana*.

Samatha differs from the Zen style in that it "pays attention to the breath leaving the nostril and dissolving into the space in front of the face." It is a process of "*re*directing your attention constantly . . .

outside of your body," which promotes "egolessness because you're meditating in the empty space into which your breath dissolves, rather than into any psychological or sensational phenomena going on inside the body."[3]

Ginsberg describes *samatha* and *vipasyana* as devices for "clearing the mind, making thoughts more transparent—so that there's not a lot of garbage there obstructing the later practices."[4] Ginsberg clothes his position in Eastern garb but voices an epistemology with discernible kinship to Eliot's "depersonalization," Williams's "objectivism," but most strikingly, Olson's "objectism," which advocated a similar ego humiliation in its insistence that poets rid themselves of the "lyrical interference of the individual as ego, of the 'subject' and his soul, that peculiar presumption by which western man has interposed himself between what he is as a creature of nature . . . and those other creatures of nature which we may, with no derogation, call objects."[5]

The *samatha-vipasyana* practice allows Ginsberg to observe "the mechanical nature of certain passions, like anger and sex, so that they become more transparent . . . When you're shouting and angry, you don't really communicate the details of what you know." Meditation helps one to "calm down, consider what would be the best way of communicating the simplest elements of facts—unprejudiced by my own anger and resentments." Not only does anger impede the attention to facts, but so does the pressure to write: "I was obsessed with writing and transforming everything into writing," Ginsberg confessed in 1975, "and that obsession was inhibiting the writing. . . . It was only conducive to a lot of mental friction, and self-consciousness, and inattentiveness to detail outside. . . . I felt that I had to write a poem all the time. That affected my seeing things because I was seeing things in terms of how you verbalize them."

Ultimately, the *samatha-vipasyana* practice led to Ginsberg's celebration of "ordinary mind" and his poetic credo "First thought, best thought" (*CP*, xx). "*Samatha* practice does help," he says, ". . . because you become more minutely aware of what's rising in the mind, thought forms rising and then disappearing. And you learn to look on them with less prejudice than before—like this thought is good and that thought's bad. Any thought will do!"[6]

What *Mind Breaths'* title more or less seems to promise, then, are poems reflecting detailed awareness, egolessness, and nonjudgmental vision. The slim volume delivers some of these qualities, but the line separating "awareness," "egolessness," and "ordinary mind" from vintage Ginsbergian polemic, prophecy, and unerotic erotica is anything but clearcut. One does sense, however, the Buddhist religious posture more insistently supplanting Ginsberg's previous cultish devotion to his death-ravaged gang of old friends—Cassady, Kerouac, Solomon, Huncke, and Burroughs.

The title poem "Mind Breaths" reenacts a *samatha-vipasyana* meditation:

Thus crosslegged on round pillow sat in Teton Space—
I breathed upon the aluminum microphone-stand a body's length away
I breathed upon the teacher's throne, the wooden chair with wooden pillow
I breathed further, past the sake cup half emptied by the breathing
    guru. . . .

                                                                     (CP, 609)

Mind-breath awareness attenuates to Idaho, the Sacramento Valley, Hawaii, Fiji, Kyoto, Cambodia, Delhi, Tel Aviv, Piraeus, Rome, Marseilles, London, Chicago, Nebraska, Denver, and back to "the cafeteria at Teton Village" where "a calm breath, a silent breath, a slow breath breathes outward from the nostrils" (CP, 611). Yes, we have nonjudgmental egolessness here, but one wonders whether the poem does not exemplify Harold Beaver's complaint that *Mind Breaths* "suggests spiritual afflatus and yoga exercises and consciousness raising . . . [but] the whole slim volume is no more than one unfiled catalogue among countless unfiled catalogues of awareness"?[7]

"Ego Confessions" (Ginsberg's *Song of Myself*) hardly seems to reflect "egolessness" with its brash opening: "I want to be known as the most brilliant man in America" (CP, 623), but by virtue of its confessional stance, it becomes an outpouring, like *Howl*, of total, unpremeditated honesty. The poem is, as Hayden Carruth observes, a mockery of confessional poetry itself, but a mockery that "transcends itself."[8] The egotistic thoughts in the poem seem even to Ginsberg an "embarrassing reality," but he had learned to appreciate as early as *Howl* that "such embarrassments always prove to be signs that something is going on." What is, in fact, "going on" in "Ego Confessions," he tells us, is "tricky . . . sort of sly," because the "extravagance" of the phenomenon was "an obviously emotional truth" that was part of the "thoughts and formulations that pass through my mind."[9] Apparently, the poem's mockery is intended to disarm us against the emotional truth it in fact asserts.

Probably the best and most attractive poem in *Mind Breaths* is "Mugging," a poetic narrative of a street assault. It is Ginsberg at his best. His detailed awareness of his neighborhood is superbly catalogued:

—Crossed the street, traffic lite red, thirteen bus roaring by liquor store,
past corner pharmacy iron grated, past Coca Cola & Mylai posters fading
   scraped on brick
Past Chinese Laundry wood door'd, & broken cement stoop steps For Rent
   hall painted green & purple Puerto Rican style. . . .

                                                (*CP*, 625)

And the passage is spiced with infallible Ginsberg humor as we hear him chant "Om Ah Hûm to gangs of lovers on the stoop watching" as he goes down under the muggers' attack. Ruefully, Ginsberg arises after the assault from "the cardboard mattress thinking Om Ah Hûm didn't stop em," rationalizing the mantra's failure with: "the tone of voice too loud" (*CP*, 626).

Street description is a choric element in this poem. Before the mugging, the visual details, despite the urban blight, are vivid and engaging. There is a "Halloween" summer sky, the stoops are filled with "gangs of lovers," and even the mugger puts "his arm around my neck / tenderly" (*CP*, 625). After the assault, however, the street becomes

a bombed-out face, building rows' eyes & teeth missing
burned apartments half the long block, gutted cellars, hallways' charred
   beams
hanging over trash plaster mounded entrances, couches & bedsprings rusty
   after sunset.

                                                (*CP*, 626)

Even the lovers have been replaced by "stoopfuls of scared kids frozen in black hair" (*CP*, 627).

All of Ginsberg's strengths are efficiently at work in this enterprise; there are energy-producing juxtapositions, meticulous catalogues of detail, dramatic ironies, and most of all Ginsberg's zany comic touch, which instantly withers the potential sentimentality that often mars his efforts.

If "Mugging" is Ginsberg at his best, the long, pretentious allergory, "Contest of Bards," is Ginsberg at his worst. The poem strains for mythic profundity by dramatizing a meeting between a failing old

prophet and a young poet, presumably on the rise, who comes to re-
mind the old bard of his youthful prophetic powers. Obscure and
melodramatic, the poem may have served Ginsberg therapeutically,
like some verbal equivalent of Yeats's monkey glands, but it reads
like an interminable, unfunny parody that, uncharacteristically for
Ginsberg, seems forced and artificial.

"Don't Grow Old," on the other hand, is a very real and moving
five-part series of poems about his father, Louis, a subject he took up
again two years later in *Plutonian Ode* in a poem bearing the same title. The portrait of Louis, the "Old Poet" whose death—"Poetry's
final subject"—"glimmers months ahead" (CP, 651), is rendered in
typically graphic detail:

Coughing up gastric saliva
Marriages vanished in a cough
Hard to get up from the easy chair
Hands white feet speckled a blue toe stomach big breasts hanging thin
hair white on chest
too tired to take off shoes and black sox.

                                                                    (CP, 651)

The sentiment is controlled:

              I read my father Wordsworth's *Intimations of*
                        Immortality
     ". . . *trailing clouds of glory do we come*
        from God, who is our home . . ."
                    "That's beautiful," he said, "but it's not true."
                                                                    (CP, 652)

But the consolation is given in almost flippant blues rhythm, and in
rhymed triplets:

                    Hey Father Death, I'm flying home
                    Hey poor man, you're all alone
                    Hey old daddy, I know where I'm going

                    Father Death, Don't cry any more
                    Mama's there, underneath the floor
                    Brother Death, please mind the store.
                                                                    (CP, 652)

"Don't Grow Old" is a kind of elegy before the fact of death and it seems to share many qualities of perceptive awareness and disciplined calm before the anxiety of death that we find in the meditation "What would you do if you lost it?" The poem was inspired by a question Trungpa, Ginsberg's guru, asked him when he saw him in his apartment lobby carrying his harmonium case. "Better prepare for Death" (*CP*, 592), says Trungpa in the poem's opening, immediately elevating the harmonium case to a symbol. The preparation for death that follows is an inventory of possessions, both material and spiritual that are meticulously itemized and then bid farewell: "Tibetan precious-metal finger cymbals. . . . The Wooden bowl from Haiti . . . bodies adored to the nipple . . . all wisdoms I never studied . . . newspaper interviews, assemblaged archives, useless paperworks surrounding me . . . Naomi . . . old painful legged poet Louis" and even "America you hope you prayer you tenderness, you IBM 135-35 Electronic Automated Battlefield Igloo White Dragon-tooth Fuel Air Bomb over Indochina" (*CP*, 592–93). A final goodbye, before the poem fades away in Buddhist chanting, is extended to "Heaven . . . Nirvana . . . sad Paradise . . . all angels and archangels, devas & devakis, Bodhisattvas, Buddhas . . ." (*CP*, 593), which suggests the poem's ultimate point: divestment of all attachments to the ego. Ginsberg once put it this way: ". . . learning non attachment to specific facets of the image of myself that I created through my poetry and through my own mind, and to my friends. Learning to break those stereotypes, allowing those stereotypes to fall apart naturally."[10] Thus the poem itself is a meditational exercise to promote a salutary "emptiness," even including periodic progress reports: "my own breath slower now, silent waiting & watching" (*CP*, 593).

In "What would you do if you lost it?" Ginsberg mentions an accident he experienced slipping on ice in Cherry Valley, New York, which accentuated his response to Trungpa's admonition, "Better prepare for Death" ("A broken leg a week later enough reminder" [*CP*, 592]). He saw that accident as "a direct object lesson that while the mind was clouded with resentment and anger, I could get hurt!" In a sense, he realized, it was not an accident at all but a consequence of his lapse of "mindfulness"; "I wasn't being careful when I was walking because I wasn't observing the ground since my eyes were rolled in my head in anger."[11] The point is interesting, for it recalls how much anger contributed to the energy of Ginsberg's early poems, *Howl* in particular. Buddhism and Trungpa clearly were effecting changes in the poet, particularly in the political area.

A case in point is "News Bulletin." Here is a political poem that touches on most of the issues Ginsberg has always felt strongly about: drugs, Abbie Hoffman, the Jewish holocaust, pornography legislation, Leary jailed, Nixon, the Vietnam war. But as he hears about them on his radio, while exercising his "painful ankle" (CP, 605), he is not roused to passionate rage but, as he himself explains it, "was comparing, realistically, my actual life with my news resentments." "Mindfulness" did not permit him to vent just anger but to include his awareness of the reality about him with that anger—neutralizing it, so to speak, into what Ginsberg calls "empty awareness." "I wasn't taking a partial account of just my resentments, my angers, and my perceptions of politics, but I was including what my real life was doing at the same time—sometimes contrasting with the so-called anger. In a sense, I was exposing my own hypocrisy, as well as the humor of the actual situation of getting angry, and, at the same time, making borscht."[12]

Perhaps this just means dealing with one's anger objectively, even dispassionately, so as to see the truth in it without distortion. Poetically, the notion of "empty awareness" translates into objectivism, which, as we know from the work of William Carlos Williams, hardly means the absence of feeling or compassion. To the contrary, says Ginsberg, "compassion is a by-product of empty awareness."[13]

Empty awareness means "neutral, benevolent, indifferent attention"[14]—a stance toward reality that is free of the ego's distorting interference. Ginsberg codifies the principle in "Manifesto," a poetic assertion that rejects belief in "Soul . . . The heart . . . immortal Ego . . . God . . . science reason reality and good moral Will . . . Democracy, Fascism, Communism and heroes" (CP, 617) in order to validate a single quality of life:

> There is Awareness—which confounds the Soul, Heart, God, Science
> Love Governments and Cause & Effects' Nightmare.

(CP, 617)

Plutonian Ode

Kaddish, Ginsberg's finest work, possesses a powerfully private appeal that sets it apart from his other major works, so that if we seek poetic benchmarks with which to measure his development as a poet of public conscience, we are better served by *Howl, Wichita Vortex Sutra,* and *Plutonian Ode. Howl* spatters us with comic extravagance and youthful outrage, a delicious, unrestrained temper tantrum that speeds us so kaleidoscopically across the cultural underbelly of fifties America that the power of its exaggerated complaints seems (for the moment, anyway) to ring true. *Wichita Vortex Sutra,* although it richly evokes a sense of America and diagnoses its illnesses with a certain compelling urgency, lacks the exhuberant speed and energy of the earlier work, causing at least one unsympathetic reviewer to complain "much of the rude honesty of Ginsberg's early work has been drained away by his subsequent thumpery. The more he has based his poetry on something other than his original exhuberance and anger, the more tenuous and desperate the howl has become."[15]

Like *Wichita Vortex Sutra,* the antinuclear *Plutonian Ode* is an exorcism, but one directed at a "Radioactive Nemesis" (*CP,* 702), plutonium, that enlists (among others) a "Homeric formula for appeasing underground millionaire Pluto Lord of Death, jack in the gnostic box of Aeons, and Adamantine Truth of ordinary mind inspiration, unhexing Nuclear ministry of fear" (*CP,* 817). Thus, it is a plutonian rather than plutonium ode, testifying to Paul Berman's charge that here Ginsberg "has scrounged up what seems like every possible element for a new nuclear language—Greek myth (Pluto, Hades, and Nemesis), Buddhism and Buddhist numerology, the exorcist formulas of his own anti-Vietnam conjurings, the language of Whitman, even what seems like a hint of Eliot, via 'Waste Land' type footnotes."[16]

It is a "literary" poem, and this, more than anything else, distinguishes it from *Howl* and *Wichita Vortex Sutra.* There is, of course, adherence to the classic form of the ode, but there are also invocations, epic genealogies, allusions galore to Williams, Whitman, Blake, the Bible, most of whom are pressed into the service of a poetic breath that, like the *samatha-vipasyana* meditation in *Mind Breaths,* becomes an "openmouthed exhaling" (*CP,* 702) that covers the vast geography of the nuclear industry stretching from the "silent mills at Hanford," through "Rocky Flats . . . Albuquerque . . . Washington, South Carolina, Colorado, Texas, Iowa, New Mexico, / where nuclear reactors create a new Thing under the Sun, where Rockwell warplants fabricate this death stuff . . ." (*CP,* 702–3). The mantra chant crescendos. Ginsberg's corporate breath hurls challenges at the "Manufactured Spectre of human reason" (*CP,* 703), which he accuses of deluding America:

I dare your Reality, I challenge your very being! I publish your cause and
    effect!
I turn the Wheel of Mind on your three hundred tons! Your name enters
    mankind's ear! I embody your ultimate powers!
My oratory advances on your vaunted Mystery! This breath dispels your
    braggart fears!

                                                              (*CP*, 703)

Entering the very "fuel rod drums" of the "Infernal Room" of the
nuclear fortress, the poem's "measured harmony floats audible," its
"jubilant tones" becoming "honey and milk and wine-sweet water,
which is ritualistically poured on the reactor's core along with syllables of "barley groats," all "to seal you up Eternally with Diamond
Truth! O doomed Plutonium" (*CP*, 704).

Steven Axelrod, who finds it impossible "not to sympathize with
the anti-nuclear sentiments of the piece," nevertheless does worry
about *Plutonian Ode* as a poem. "It is a sign of what goes wrong," he
says, "that the poem comes equipped with twenty-two notes identify-
ing sources and interpreting difficult lines for slow readers," and then
goes on to complain that the poem "devolves to mere 'oratory,' as
Ginsberg himself calls it." It also devolves, he continues, "into a parody of William Blake and Walt Whitman," which leads to his intriguing conclusion that "resorting to the paraphernalia of academic
scholarship in 'Plutonian Ode,' Ginsberg has become, willy-nilly, the
Columbia University English professor he was genetically and socially
programmed to be. Anyone who has heard his magnificently learned
and boring lectures on Blake at the Naropa Institute will understand
that argument. But I think it is more likely that Ginsberg's new self-
important demeanor in both his work and his life—his elder statesman, poet laureate Tennyson-in-the-Rockies persona—is simply a
way of disguising from us and from himself the slow extinguishment
of his utterance."[17]

Perhaps he was programmed for Columbia, but Ginsberg's professional talents eventually settled elsewhere, as he wryly documents for
us in "Brooklyn College Brain":

> You used to wear dungarees & blue workshirt,
> sneakers or cloth-top shoes, & ride alone
> on subways, young & elegant unofficial
> bastard of nature, sneaking sweetness into Brooklyn.

> Now tweed jacket & yr father's tie on yr breast,
> salmon-pink cotton shirt & Swedish bookbag
> you're half bald, palsied lip & lower eyelid
> continually tearing, gone back to college.
>
> (*CP*, 717)

It is hard to feel the "self-important demeanor" that Axelrod detected in *Plutonian Ode* here, but Ginsberg does seem to render a jolting collision between what he once was ("unofficial bastard of nature") and what he senses he has become ("Professor Ginsberg"). In fact, there is a rueful irony in the poem's next lines:

> Goodbye Professor Ginsberg, get your identity
> card next week from the front office so you can
> get to class without being humiliated dumped on the
> sidewalk by the black guard at the Student Union door.
>
> (*CP*, 717)

If, as Kenneth Funsten says, "Ginsberg has become in the popular imagination a sort of cranky old hippie, a bead-carrying guru friend of Bob Dylan and Mick Jagger,"[18] it would seem from "Brooklyn College Brain" that he may feel more comfortable in that role than as professor, elder statesman, or poet laureate. Even so, many of the poems in *Plutonian Ode* reflect a frankly pathetic self-doubt underlying the public front.

"Grim Skeleton," for example, depicts a sick and disconsolate Ginsberg amid his newspaper clippings ("Library of my own deeds of mu- ·sic tongue & oratoric yell") wondering what it is that has brought him to this spiritual cul-de-sac. "Is it my heart, a cold & phlegm in my skull or radiator / Comfort cowardice," he asks himself, or "Is it the guru of music or guru of meditation whose harsh force I bear . . .?" He speaks disgustedly of his "yatter of meditation," his "pro- phetic fake manuscripts," and wonders if he has unconsciously sold out to the very forces he has opposed for so long:

> . . . am I myself the CIA
> bought with acid meat & alcohol in Washington, silenced in meditation
> on my own duplicity. . . .
>
> (*CP*, 690)

Most of all, he seems distressed by the realization of the "Fantasy of Fame / I dreamt in adolescence" that "Came true last week over Television." Has success spoiled Allen Ginsberg? he asks himself. "What's my sickness, flu virus or Selfhood infected swollen sore . . . Whose sucker am I" (*CP*, 690–91).

Self-deprecation speaks unabashedly in "Ode to Failure" where Ginsberg intones a litany of personal defeats:

My tirades destroyed no Intellectual Unions of KGB & CIA in turtlenecks
    & underpants, their woolen suits and tweeds . . .
I never dissolved Plutonium or dismantled the nuclear Bomb before my skull
    lost hair
I have not yet stopped the Armies of entire Mankind in their march toward
    World War III
I never got to Heaven, Nirvana, X, Whatchamacallit, I never left Earth,
I never learned to die.

(CP, 737)

Self-pity speaks out frankly in a series of love poems in this volume. "Lacklove" shows us an aging lover who lies alone and rejected while

> a desired youthful lover won't in truth
> Come to bed with me, instead
> Loves the thoughts inside my head.
> (*CP*, 693)

Less morose, "Love Returned" recounts an unexpected visit of another (perhaps the same) lover, but even here, the joy is incomplete: "Alas for my dreams / my part's feeble it seems" (*CP*, 713). In "Some Love" the dilemma is more pronounced:

> Rarer and rarer
> Boys give me favor
> Older and Older
> Love grows bolder.
> (*CP*, 722)

And in "Maybe Love" the theme reaches its sad culmination:

> Maybe love will come
> cause I am not so dumb
> Tonight it fills my heart

> heavy sad apart
> from one or two I fancy
> now I'm an old fairy.
>
> (*CP*, 723)

What is interesting about these love poems is their return to conventional form—even stanzas, rhymed couplets, and iambic cadence, for the most part—quite a change from Melvillian bardic breath, but perhaps appropriate to theme in the sense that so many of the poems in *Plutonian Ode* seem to contrast ebullience of youth with the various accommodations forced by age.

Some may find the political poems "Birdbrain!" and "Capitol Air" important evocations of social outrage, but for most, they will seem sad, vastly inferior specimens of warmed-over *Howl*. They employ the familiar Ginsberg device of fashioning a bottomless container for all the eclectic complaints he can think of. In "Birdbrain!" it is the vocative "Birdbrain" itself:

> Birdbrain runs the world!
> Birdbrain is the ultimate product of Capitalism
> Birdbrain chief bureaucrat of Russia, yawning. . . .
>
> (*CP*, 738)

In "Capitol Air" it is the even simpler "I don't like":

> I don't like the government where I live
> I don't like dictatorship of the Rich
> I don't like bureaucrats telling me what to eat. . . .
>
> (*CP*, 743)

The complaints and name-calling are not of sufficient sophistication, substance, or interest to overcome the monotony of the form, and the poems come off as rather sophomoric litanies that cast some doubt on the validity of the principle "First thought, best thought."

The best poems in *Plutonian Ode* are of the quiet, descriptive, private sort. "Manhattan May Day Midnight" (*CP*, 718) is effective simply because of its vividly gritty description, and "Garden State" juxtaposes the past and present of Ginsberg's New Jersey in an effectively detailed time collage. The best, however, is another version of "Don't Grow Old." Relentlessly unsentimental and relentlessly honest, this poem is as touching a reminiscence of a father-son relationship as one could want. And graphic, too:

We lifted his swollen feet talcum'd white, put them thru pajama legs,
tied the cord round his waist, and held the nightshirt sleeve open for his
    hand, slow.
Mouth drawn in, his false teeth in a dish, he turned his head round
looking up at Peter to smile ruefully, "Don't ever grow old."

(*CP,* 710)

Chapter Nine

Conclusion

Ginsberg explains in *Collected Poems: 1947–1980* that the poetry in this volume has been "rearranged in straight chronological order to compose an autobiography" (*CP,* xix), forcefully serving notice that the Ginsberg life, not the Ginsberg canon, holds priority. Since, as Harold Beaver expresses it, "Ginsberg has no privacies. Or rather he is all privacies . . . a perpetual fountainhead of his inner life."[1] his work is in fact "a relentless self-exposure,"[2] a public diary. Here, then, is no collection of poems as poems but rather poems as life and, perhaps more to the point, life as poems, for rarely is a Ginsberg poem merely referential to experience, but, at its best, experience itself. When experience is pronounced holy, as it is in Ginsberg's credo, and when he vows: "I want to be a saint, a real saint when I am still young,"[3] we acknowledge his work as special. This is not merely to class Ginsberg as a Romantic or even a confessional poet (of course he is both) but to assert, on the grounds that his life is a work of art, that *Collected Poems* amounts to nothing less than an autohagiography.

Ginsberg is not everyone's saint, of course, and here is where literary criticism has run into shoals when it assays his art. Denied the privilege of separating form from content (Ginsberg's art from his life), the critic, to be fair, must address the whole ball of wax: the drugs, the brilliance, the politics, the homosexuality, the psychopathology, the mysticism, the self-pity, the silliness—in a word, the complete Ginsberg. Before such a circumstance, conventional literary judgment (is this a good or bad poem?) finds itself "shanghaied" from a safely aesthetic to a dangerously moral context (is this a good man or bad man?). Such category mixing spells the death of literary judgment.

Obviously, Ginsberg's "lifelong poem" (*CP,* xxi) is no meat for New Critics or for any breed of absolutists. It was written in and for a contemporary pluralist culture that itself is in the throes of searching for new ways of understanding and addressing reality. It is a postmodernist world that is experiencing, as Ginsberg puts it, "the drama

of breakthrough from closed form to open form in American poetry"
(*CP,* xxi).

Just as the young Ginsberg had to open his life by facing and con-
quering shame, so in his poetry we see a parallel opening from the
constraining rigidities of conventional prosody to "Hebraic-Melvillean
bardic breath." Open form, particularly as its arch theoretician,
Charles Olson, developed the idea, is more than a literary strategy; it
is a comprehensive stance toward reality, which meshes perfectly with
Ginsberg's eventual gravitation to Buddhism.

The aim of open form in poetry is liberation from the epistemological constraints of "literacy." "It's very crucial today to be sure that
you stay illiterate," Olson once said, "simply because literacy is
wholly dangerous, so dangerous that I'm involved everytime I read
poetry, in the fact that I'm reading to people who are literate—and
they are *not* hearing. They may be listening with all their minds, but
they don't hear."[4] What they don't hear is what Ginsberg has termed
the "undifferentiated consciousness,"[5] and what for Olson was "the
world of complex simultaneity."[6] Olson blames people's deafness to
these primary realities on the Greeks: "We stay unaware how two
means of discourse the Greeks appear to have invented [logic and clas-
sification] hugely intermit our participation in our experience, and so
prevent discovery. . . . [They have made] a "universe" out of discourse instead of letting it rest in its most serviceable places . . .
logos and the reason necessary to it, are only a stage which a man
must master and not what they are taken to be, a final discipline.
Beyond them is direct perception and the contraries which dispose of
argument."[7] Ginsberg's incessant pursuit of spiritual, intellectual,
and physical nakedness is simply his personal version of a broader
postmodernist quest for open forms that liberate literary art from a
"universe of discourse" into a truly "human universe" of "direct perception and contraries."

From the point of view of one who considers the poet a "maker"
or craftsman of "discrete" poems that thereupon become available for
analysis, interpretation, and criticism, Ginsberg's open forms will
seem perverse, for they reject the overt manipulation of reality that
such words as *craft* and *art* imply. Fealty to the real is the overriding
criterion. Postmodernist artists and theoreticians often allude to Wer-
ner Heisenberg's "uncertainty principle" as a kind of scientific rationale for avoiding artifice, pointing out that just as the instruments of
observation in physics distort the reality of the observed phenomenon

(we must "freeze" mass to weigh it, and mass is never in repose), so in verse the intrusion of literary "devices" artificially stops the ongoing process of continuous reality. In short, Ginsberg's notions of "ordinary mind" and "First thought, best thought" are "projective" in the sense that they assume an attitude of passive obedience to the inner and outer experiences he registers.

Perhaps the greatest burden of patience falls on the readers of open poetry, for they, even more than the poets (who at least have the guidance of their own experiences to assist them) are truly "naked" in the open field. They are advised that an open poem is a reenactment rather than an artifact and that they should concern themselves with absorbing the energies (rather than substance) that are "held" in a kind of dynamic tension within the field of the poem. The images of the poem, by virtue of the solidity that breath gives them, are allowed the free play of their individual energies, they are advised, even while, through juxtaposition with other images, they create an energy field. The character of the engagement that readers are expected to have is radically different from that with which they are accustomed. They are asked to "avoid all irritable reaching after fact and reason" and to remain in "empty awareness," or as Olson would say, "in the absolute condition of present things"[8]—that is, in the poem itself.

Notes and References

Preface

    1. John Tytell, *Naked Angels: The Lives & Literature of the Beat Generation* (New York: McGraw-Hill, 1976), 104.
    2. William Logan, *TLS,* 12 November 1982, 1251.
    3. William A. Henry III, "In New York *Howl* Becomes a Hoot," *Time,* 7 December 1981; reprinted in *On the Poetry of Allen Ginsberg,* ed. Lewis Hyde (Ann Arbor: University of Michigan Press, 1984), 369.

Chapter One

    1. Paul Portugés, *The Visionary Poetics of Allen Ginsberg* (Santa Barbara, Calif.: Ross-Erikson, 1978), xiv.
    2. Note this stanza from *Howl:*

who studied Plotinus Poe St. John of the Cross telepathy and bop kaballa
    because the cosmos instinctively vibrated at their feet in Kansas. . . .
                                               (*CP,* 127)

    3. Quoted in Alan W. Watts, *Beat Zen, Square Zen, and Zen* (San Francisco: City Lights Books, 1959), 22.
    4. John P. Sisk, "Beatniks and Tradition." *Commonweal.* 17 April 1959, 76.
    5. Paul O'Neil, "The Only Rebellion Around," *Life,* 30 November 1959, 115.
    6. Carl Michalson, "What Is Existentialism?" in *Christianity and the Existentialists,* ed. Carl Michalson (New York: Scribners, 1956), 13.
    7. Thomas Clark, "The Art of Poetry VIII," *Paris Review* 37 (Spring 1966): 42–43.
    8. Jack Kerouac, "The Origins of the Beat Generation," *Playboy,* June 1959, 32.
    9. Gary Snyder, "Note on the Religious Tendencies," *Liberation,* June 1959, 11.
    10. Kerouac, "Origins of the Beat Generation," 42.
    11. See Portugés, *Visionary Poetics,* for a full treatment of this experience, in addition to Ginsberg's own account excerpted ahead.
    12. Clark, "Art of Poetry VIII," 36–37. "Psalm IV" (*CP,* 238) is Ginsberg's poetic rendering of his "secret vision" of Blake.

13. Quoted in Alan W. Watts, *The Way of Zen* (New York: Mentor, 1959), 116.

14. Watts, *Beat Zen*, 3.

15. " 'First thought, best thought.' Spontaneous insight—the sequence of thought-forms passing naturally through ordinary mind—was always motif and method of these compositions" ("Author's Preface, Reader's Manual," *CP*, xx).

16. Portugés, *Visionary Poetics*, 161–62.

17. Ibid. 122.

18. Watts, *Beat Zen*, 9.

19. Watts, *Way of Zen*, 40.

20. Peter Chowka, Interview with Ginsberg, *New Age Journal*, April 1976; reprinted in *Poetry of Ginsberg*, ed. Hyde, 320.

21. Quoted by Francis X. Clines, "Allen Ginsberg: Intimations of Mortality," *New York Times Magazine*, 11 November 1984, 92.

22. Quoted in Richard Kostelanetz, "Ginsberg Makes the World Scene," *New York Times*, 11 July 1965, sec. 4, 27.

23. Paul Christensen reports that "the outcast version of himself came to him in a dream . . . a monster of instinctual desire who has been rejected by society" ("Allen Ginsberg," *Dictionary of Literary Biography*, Vol. 16 [Detroit: Gale Research Co., 1983], 217).

24. According to Tytell, "When a chambermaid reported that 'Fuck the Jews' and 'Nicholas Murray Butler has no balls' had been inscribed on the dirty film of Ginsberg's window, Dean of Students McKnight was outraged and wanted Ginsberg expelled" (*Naked Angels*, 85).

25. Kostelanetz, "Ginsberg," 28.

26. According to Harold Beaver's characterization, "Ginsberg was the big city shepherd to this intellectual sucker from Denver. Cassady was the moronic adolescent to the Faustian father, apprentice to professional poet, Goy to Jew, Dedalus to Bloom" (Review of *Mind Breaths*, *TLS*, 7 July 1978, 754).

27. In the notes to *CP*, Ginsberg specifies that four poems ("A Further Proposal," "A Lover's Garden," "Love Letter," and "Dakar Doldrums") were "dedicated to Neal Cassady in the first years of our friendship, [and] were set among 'Earlier Poems: 1947,' appended to *Gates of Wrath*, a book of rhymed verse" (*CP*, 749–56).

28. Beaver, 754.

29. Diana Trilling, "The Other Night at Columbia," *Partisan Review* (Spring, 1959); reprinted in *Poetry of Ginsberg*, ed. Hyde, 58.

30. Paul Carroll, "*Playboy* Interview," *Playboy*, April 1969, 86.

31. "Friend and early contact for Kerouac, Burroughs and the author [Ginsberg] in explorations circa 1945 around Times Square, where he hung out at center of the hustling world in early stages of his opiate addictions.

. . . Huncke introduced Burroughs and others to the slang, information and ritual of the emergent 'hip' or 'beat' subculture" (Ginsberg's note [*CP*, 758]).

32. Ginsberg identified Peter Orlovsky as his "wife" in the biographical fact sheet he was invited to submit to *Who's Who*.

33. See *The Yage Letters* [with William Burroughs] (San Francisco: City Lights Books, 1963).

34. See Timothy Leary's account of Ginsberg's experience "under the mushroom" in "In the Beginning, Leary Turned on Ginsberg and Saw That It Was Good," in *Poetry of Ginsberg,* ed. Hyde, 231–39.

35. Hyde, ed. *Poetry of Ginsberg,* 6.

36. Carroll, *"Playboy* Interview," 236.

37. Ibid., 237.

38. Helen Vendler, "A Lifelong Poem Including History," *New Yorker,* 13 January 1986, 83.

39. Les Berton, "Allen Ginsberg: No Longer Howling in the Wilderness," *Wall Street Journal,* 11 March 1986, 28.

40. Quoted in David Remnick, "The World & Allen Ginsberg," *Washington Post,* 17 March 1985, K4.

41. All quotations ibid.

Chapter Two

1. Nancy Bunge, "How Can You Teach Poetry If You Don't Sing the Blues," *Washington Post,* 29 July 1984, C3.

2. "I thought high-class poetry meant something besides just ordinary mind," said Ginsberg in a 1984 interview, "Trying to fake another kind of mind or language or perception constantly leads poets into paradoxical situations when they fake something that might be imitatively interesting, but [which] ultimately is uninteresting to them" (in ibid). See also Ginsberg's remarks on "ordinary mind" quoted in Chapter One, n. 43.

3. Charles Olson, "The Human Universe," *Human Universe and Other Essays,* ed. Donald Allen (New York: Grove Press, 1967), 3–4.

4. "Dawn," *Chicago Review,* 12 (Spring 1958): 8.

5. William Burroughs, *The New Writing in the U.S.A.,* ed. Donald Allen and Robert Creeley (Harmondsworth, England: Penguin, 1967), 20.

6. Walt Whitman, *Song of Myself,* in *Complete Poetry and Selected Prose,* ed. James E. Miller, Jr. (Boston: Houghton Mifflin Co., 1959), 38.

7. A. R. Ammons, "Ginsberg's New Poems," *Poetry* 104 (June 1964):186–87.

8. Robert Duncan, quoted in Burroughs, *New Writing,* 18.

9. Clark, "Art of Poetry VIII," 21.

10. The words originally are Robert Creeley's, but they were incorpo-

rated by Charles Olson into his famous essay "Projective Verse," *Human Universe*, 52.

11. Karl Shapiro, *A Primer for Poets* (Lincoln: University of Nebraska Press, 1953), 46.

12. Clark, "Art of Poetry VIII," 28–29.

13. Erich Auerbach, *Mimesis,* trans. Willard Trask (Princeton, N.J.: Princeton University Press, 1953), 1–20.

14. Bunge, "How Can You Teach," C3.

15. Olson, *Human Universe,* 52.

16. *The Indian Journals: March 1962–May 1963* San Francisco: Dave Haselwood and City Lights Books, 1970), 156–57.

17. I refer here to Charles Olson's review essay "Equal, That Is, to the Real Itself," *Human Universe,* 117–22, in which Olson spells out the ontological justification for nonmimetic poetry.

18. Paul Geneson, "A Conversation with Allen Ginsberg," *Chicago Review* 27 (Summer 1975):28.

19. Those familiar with the work of J. L. Austin will recognize the presence of his concept of "performative language"—language that (like the bridegroom's "I do") *does* what it says. See *How To Do Things with Words,* ed. J. O. Urmson (Cambridge: Cambridge University Press, 1962).

20. *Indian Journals,* 38–39.

21. The words are Olson's, *Human Universe,* 118.

22. "This is specifically what we've been doing—the whole poetry revolution. Williams's whole point was to return to the oral tradition to actual speech, to make it possible to talk again, *for real"* (Alison Colbert, "A Talk with Allen Ginsberg," *Partisan Review* 38 [Autumn 1971]:307).

23. I. A. Richards, *Mencius on the Mind* (London: Routledge & Kegan Paul, 1964), 8.

24. See Jane Harrison, *Ancient Art and Ritual* (London: Thornton Butterworth, 1913), 35.

25. Ibid, p. 35.

26. Colbert, "Talk with Ginsberg," 295.

27. William Carlos Williams, *I Wanted to Write a Poem,* ed. Edith Heal (Boston: Beacon Press, 1958), 15.

28. Olson, *Human Universe,* 54.

29. William Carlos Williams, "Essay on *Leaves of Grass,*" in *Leaves of Grass One Hundred Years After,* ed. Milton Hindus (Stanford: Stanford University Press, 1955), 23.

30. Olson, *Human Universe,* 52.

31. "Notes Written on Finally Recording *Howl* (Fantasy Records, 1959). Repr. in Thomas Parkinson, *A Casebook On the Beats* (New York: Thomas Y. Crowell, 1961).

32. Clark, "Art of Poetry VIII," 22.

33. "Notes on *Howl*," 27.

34. Interview in Portugés, *Visionary Poetics*, 117.

35. John Tytell suggests that Ginsberg may have enjoyed a "legacy of surrealism" from André Breton who sought a " 'monologue spoken as rapidly as possible without any interruption on the part of the cerebral faculties, a monologue consequently unencumbered by the slightest inhibition and which was as closely as possible akin to spoken thought.' This 'psycho automatism' proposed to express the mind's actual functioning in the absence of controls like reason, or any superimposed moral or ethical concern" ("The Legacy of Surrealism," *Poetry of Ginsberg,* ed. Hyde, 172).

36. See Clark, "Art of Poetry VIII," 52–53.

37. Jack Kerouac, "Essentials of Spontaneous Prose," *Evergreen Review* 2 (Summer 1958) 72.

38. "Notes on *Howl,* 27.

39. Clark, "Art of Poetry VIII," 20.

40. Interview in Portugés, *Visionary Poetics,* 161–62.

41. Kerouac, "Essentials," 72.

42. John Ciardi, "Epitaph for Dead Beats," *Saturday Review,* 6 February 1960, 13.

43. Watts, *Beat Zen,* 12.

44. Ciardi, "Epitaph," 12.

45. Francis Golffing and Barbara Gibbs, "The Public Voice: Remarks on Poetry Today—The Reality of Verse," *Commentary* 28 (July 1959):67–68.

46. Carl Michalson, *The Rationality of Faith* (New York: Scribners, 1963), 117.

47. Interview in Portugés, *Visionary Poetics,* 116.

48. Ibid., 91.

49. Bunge, "How Can You Teach," C3.

50. Mark Shechner, "The Survival of Allen Ginsberg," *Partisan Review* 1 (1979); reprinted in *Poetry of Ginsberg,* ed. Hyde, 332–33.

51. Colbert, "Talk with Ginsberg," 300.

52. Schechner, "Survival," 333.

Chapter Three

1. Christensen, "Allen Ginsberg," 221.

2. "Like so many of the poems of this period," says Portugés, "['I dwelled in Hell"} is Elizabethan and metaphysical, reflecting the influence of his early models, Wyatt, Marvell, and Surrey. The poem is decorative, overwritten, full of conceits and poetic diction, with frequent reference to angels, infernos, and even a 'blazing stair'— . . . Ginsberg would later characterize this phase of his writing as 'overwritten coy stanzas, a little after Marvell, a little after Wyatt' " *(Visionary Poetics, 27).*

3. John Ower, "Allen Ginsberg," *Dictionary of Literary Biography*, Vol. 5 (Detroit: Gale Research Co., 1980), 272–73.

4. Portugés, *Visionary Poetics*, 27.

5. "A Further Proposal"; "A Lover's Garden"; "Love Letter"; "Dakar Doldrums" (*CP*, 749–56).

6. Clark, "Art of Poetry VIII," 37.

7. Ibid. 49.

8. Ibid., 48.

9. André Breton quoted by Tytell, *Naked Angels*, 228.

10. Clark, "Art of Poetry VIII," 37.

11. Paul Tillich, "Existentialist Aspects of Modern Art," in *Christianity and the Existentialists*, ed. Carl Michalson (New York: Scribners, 1956), 137.

12. See Clark, "Art of Poetry VIII," 30.

13. Quoted by Ginsberg in ibid., 28.

14. See Ian Ramsey, *Religious Language: an Empirical Placing of Theological Phrases* (London: Victor Gollancz, 1946).

15. Clark, "Art of Poetry VIII," 30.

16. Quoted in Burroughs, *New Writing*, 20.

17. Tillich, "Existentialist Aspects," 137.

18. "My intention was to *catalyze* the world, to catalyze my perceptions so that I would see trees—like in my poem, 'The Trembling of the Veil'— as live organisms on the moon!" (Portugés, *Visionary Poetics*, 111).

19. Robert Hazel, *Nation*, 11 November 1961, 381.

20. Marianne Moore writes in a letter to Ginsberg (4 July 1952): "The brick-layers' lunch hour is fine work, accurate, contagious—even if it is William C. Williams instead of (or as well as) Allen Ginsberg" (in *Poetry of Ginsberg*, ed. Hyde, 14).

21. Clark, "Art of Poetry VIII," 41.

22. Ibid., 38–39.

23. Ibid., 40.

24. Portugés, *Visionary Poetics*, 45–46, quotes a poem included in a letter Ginsberg wrote to Mark Van Doren that appears to confirm Ginsberg's belief that Blake's spirit was asking him to die:

> Die, Die, the spirit cried
> without
> Die, Die
> I cannot die
> Cry out, Cry out
> I cannot cry.

25. Portugés, *Visionary Poetics*, 115.

26. Ibid., 116.

27. Whitman, *Song of Myself,* in *Complete Poetry,* 40–41.
28. Wallace Stevens, "The Comedian as the Letter C," pt. 1, ll. 1–4.
29. A measure of the extent of this derailment can be gauged by noting this portion of a letter from Williams to Norman MacLeod: "When I say, and some well-meaning critic attacks my intelligence for saying it, that art has nothing to do with metaphysics—I am aiming at the very core of the matter. Art is some sort of honest answer, the forms of art, the discovery of the new in art forms—but to mix that with metaphysics is the prime intellectual offense of my day" (William Carlos Williams, *Selected Essays* [New York: New Directions, 1954], 238–39).
30. "In the opening piece [of *Empty Mirror*] . . ." Marianne Moore wrote to Ginsberg, "you say, 'I wandered off in search of a toilet.' And I go with you, remember. Do I have to? I do if you take me with you in your book" ("Letter to Ginsberg," 13).
31. When Ginsberg was asked by Allen Young: "Did you experience any kind of split between your hipster circle and getting involved with other gay people as you were coming out?" Ginsberg replied that the experience was recorded in his poem "In Society" (*CP,* 3). Ginsberg explains, "There were a whole group of queens around Columbia at that time who were doing things like going down to hear Edith Piaf sing at the Plaza Hotel and interested in status and money. They had cultural interests that went back to Lotte Lenya and things like that, but at the same time it was an overly aristocratic, elitist thing" (*Gay Sunshine Interview* [Bolinas, Calif.: Grey Fox Press, 1974], 4–5).
32. For an interesting discussion of the surreal features of this poem, see Tytell, *Naked Angels,* 227–35.
33. Nikolai Berdyaev, *Dream and Reality: An Essay in Autobiography;* reprinted in *A Casebook on Existentialism,* ed. William V. Spanos (New York, Crowell, 1966), 321–22.

Chapter Four

1. Kenneth Rexroth, *Assays* (New York: New Directions, 1961), 194.
2. Lawrence Ferlinghetti, "Horn on *Howl,*" *Evergreen Review* 4, (1957):155.
3. Quoted from the *San Francisco Chronicle* in ibid., 145.
4. Ibid., 146.
5. Ibid. 147.
6. Ferlinghetti, "Horn on *Howl,*" 145–58. Included also are statements given by: Kenneth Patchen; Northern California Booksellers Association; Barney Rosset and Donald Allen, editors of the *Evergreen Review,* as well as the actual statements during the trial of Mark Schorer, Leo Lowenthal,

Herbert Blau, Vincent McHugh, Mark Linenthal, and Kenneth Rexroth. Excerpts follow in the text.

7. Carroll, *"Playboy* Interview," 90.

8. Henry, "In New York," 368.

9. "Notes on *Howl,"* 28.

10. Carroll, *"Playboy* Interview," 88.

11. Clark, "Art of Poetry VIII," 15.

12. Ibid., 15–16.

13. "Poetry, Violence, and the Trembling Lambs," *Village Voice,* 25 August 1959, 8.

14. Ibid.

15. "Notes on *Howl,"* 28.

16. Gay Wilson Allen, "Walt Whitman: The Search for a 'Democratic' Structure," *Walt Whitman Handbook* (Chicago: Packard and Co., 1946); reprinted in *Discussions of Poetry: Form and Structure* (Boston: D. C. Heath & Co.: 1964), 71.

17. Ibid. 63.

18. E. C. Ross, "Whitman's Verse," *Modern Language Notes* 45 (June 1930):363–64.

19. "Notes on *Howl,"* 28–29.

20. See Ernest Fenollosa, *The Chinese Written Character as a Medium for Poetry,* ed. Ezra Pound (San Francisco: City Lights Books, 1936), 12.

21. Clark, "Art of Poetry VIII," 28.

22. "Notes on *Howl,"* 28.

23. Clark, "Art of Poetry VIII," 23–24.

24. Ibid.

25. Ibid. 24.

26. This point is explained by Ginsberg in Clark, "Art of Poetry VIII," 40.

27. "Notes on *Howl,"* 29.

28. Ibid.

29. Clark, "Art of Poetry VIII," 53.

30. Ibid.

31. Watts, *Way of Zen,* 176. Further references in this chapter follow in the text.

32. The similarity of the theme in this poem and "Wales Visitation" *(CP,* 480), written twelve years later, is striking.

33. Quoted in Watts, *Way of Zen,* 187.

Chapter Five

1. Quoted in *The New York Times,* 11 July 1965, sec. 6, 90.

2. Harvey Shapiro, "Exalted Lament," *Midstream,* Autumn 1961; reprinted in *Poetry of Ginsberg,* ed. Hyde, 89.

3. Robert Anton Wilson, review of *Kaddish, Liberation,* November 1962; reprinted in *Poetry of Ginsberg,* ed. Hyde, 86–97.

4. In his review of *Kaddish* in *Jewish Exponent,* 10 November 1961, Mortimer J. Cohen charges Ginsberg with an "illegitimate use of Jewish Tradition. . . . Speak the word Kaddish to any Jew—of high or low degree on the intellectual scale—and it bears a definite meaning. It is the hymn of praise to God for the gift of life; is the assertion of faith in God as a God of love and justice; and all this despite Death in whose presence all man and his works seem so futile and transient. . . . But in Ginsberg's *Kaddish,*—powerful as the poem is and deeply moving as its many passages are—there is a total absence of any spiritual quality that in the slightest way warrants the use of the word Kaddish" (reprinted in *Poetry of Ginsberg,* ed. Hyde, 101).

5. Clark, "Art of Poetry VIII," 49.

6. Ibid., 49–50.

7. Ibid., 24.

8. Ibid., 47.

9. Ginsberg sent a copy of *Howl* to Naomi when she was in the mental hospital and was surprised to receive a letter of eerie clarity in reply written apparently a day before she died. These words of maternal advice are quoted from that letter.

10. Clark, "Art of Poetry VIII," 39.

11. Ibid., 37–38.

12. Ibid., 40.

13. Ibid., 38.

14. Bunge, "How Can You Teach," C3.

15. *Kaddish and Other Poems 1958–1960* (San Francisco: City Lights Books, 1961), 100.

16. Erich Fromm, *Psychoanalysis and Religion* (New Haven, Yale University Press, 1959), 23.

17. Paul Tillich, *Dynamics of Faith* (New York: Harper Torchbook, 1957), 9.

18. Ginsberg used drugs in order to attain a sense of inner consciousness, which he later discovered could be achieved naturally through meditation: "What I would propose is using actual meditation to get high, to regain consciousness, to either supplement the drugs with meditation, to replace the drugs with meditation, or to augment the meditation with drugs, but to make the meditation the backbone of both political and consciousness exploration activity as a necessary ritual stabilizing influence in any kind of action" (Colbert, "Talk with Ginsberg," 303).

19. Clark, "Art of Poetry VIII," 45.

20. *The Poems of John Donne,* ed. H. J. C. Grierson, 2d ed., 2 vols. (Oxford: Oxford University Press, 1951), 1:369.

21. Interview in Portugés, *Visionary Poetics,* 121.

22. Letter to William Burroughs dated 10 June 1960 from Pucallpa, Peru; reprinted in *The Yage Letters*, 51.

23. Ibid., 52.

24. Clark, "Art of Poetry VIII," 48.

25. Ibid., 47.

26. Shapiro, *Primer for Poets*, 59–60.

Chapter Six

1. William Burroughs, "Deposition: Testimony Concerning a Sickness," *Evergreen Review* 4 (January–February 1960):15.

2. Letter from Ginsberg to author, 22 November 1966.

3. Carroll, *"Playboy* Interview," 90.

4. William Carlos Williams, *Paterson* (New York: New Directions, 1963), 77.

5. John Ciardi, "How Free Is Verse," *Saturday Review,* 11 October 1958, 38.

6. Williams, *I Wanted to Write a Poem,* 92.

7. Watts, *Way of Zen,* 173. See also the discussion of "Wales Visitation" in Chapter Seven.

8. John MacQuarrie, *Studies in Christian Existentialism* (Philadelphia: Westminster Press, 1965), 48–49.

9. Clark, "Art of Poetry VIII." 40.

10. Ibid., 22.

11. Whitman, *Song of Myself,* in *Complete Poetry,* 26.

12. James Scully, review of *Reality Sandwiches, Nation,* 16 November 1963, 330.

13. Whitman, *Song of Myself,* in *Complete Poetry,* 38.

14. Ibid., 29.

15. *TLS,* Review of *Reality Sandwiches,* 20 September 1963, 706.

16. Norman MacCaig, "Poemburgers," *New Statesman,* 5 July 1963, 20.

17. Ibid.

18. Ibid.

19. Scully, review, 330.

20. George Poulet, *Studies in Human Time* (New York: Harper Torchbook, 1959), 342.

21. Whitman, *The Complete Poetry and Prose,* ed. M. Cowley (New York: Viking, 1948), 2:92.

22. Ibid., 1:249.

23. *TLS,* 20 September 1963, 706.

24. Scully, review, 330.

25. Whitman, *Song of Myself,* in *Collected Poetry,* 42.

Chapter Seven

1. Clark, "Art of Poetry VIII," 45.
2. See Helen Vendler, review of *Planet News, New York Times Book Review,* 31 August 1969, 8.
3. Carroll, *"Playboy* Interview," 242.
4. See John Tytell, "Conversation with Allen Ginsberg," *Partisan Review* 2 (1974):256.
5. Paul Zweig, review of *Planet News, Nation,* (March 1969); reprinted in *Poetry of Ginsberg,* ed. Hyde, 197.
6. *To Eberhart from Ginsberg* (Lincoln, Mass.: Penman Press, 1976); reprinted in *Poetry of Ginsberg,* ed. Hyde, 319.
7. Clark, "Art of Poetry VIII," 48.
8. *The Yage Letters,* 52.
9. Ibid., 55.
10. Ibid., 60.
11. The kinetic basis of Olson's poetic theory is rooted in a "feedback" relation with nature: "Man's action . . . (when it is good) is the equal of all intake plus all transposing. . . . It is the equal of its cause only when it proceeds unbroken from the threshold of a man through him and back out again, without loss of quality, to the external world from which it came" (*Human Universe,* 10–11.)
12. Interview in Portugés, *Visionary Poetics,* 122.
13. Ibid., 121.
14. See Charles Olson, *Additional Prose,* ed. George Butterick (Bolinas, Calif.: Four Seasons Foundation, 1974), 17.
15. Portugés, *Visionary Poetics,* 117.
16. Ibid., 122.
17. "First Party at Ken Kesey's with Hell's Angels," has, in fact, been included in Donald Hall's introduction to poetry text *To Read Poetry* (New York: Holt Rinehart & Winston, 1982), 26–27.
18. See Roy Harvey Pearce, *The Continuity of American Poetry* (Princeton, N.J.: Princeton University Press, 1961), 83.
19. Helen Vendler, review of *The Fall of America, New York Times Book Review,* 7 April 1973; reprinted in *Poetry of Ginsberg,* ed. Hyde, 206.
20. *Indian Journals,* 38–39.
21. The phrase is Vendler's, review of *Fall,* 207.
22. See *CP,* 815.
23. See William H. Pritchard, review of *The Fall of America, Hudson Review* 26 (Autumn 1973):593.
24. Paul Carroll, *The Poem in Its Skin* (Chicago: Big Table, 1969) reprinted in *Poetry of Ginsberg,* ed. Hyde, 294–95.
25. Ibid., 300.

26. . . . not that mu-sick (the trick
    of corporations, newspapers, slick magazines, movie houses,
    the ships, even the wharves, absentee-owned
    they whine to my people, these entertainers, sellers
    they play upon their bigotries (upon the fears. . . .
(Charles Olson, *The Maximus Poems* [New York: Jargon/Corinth, 1960],
10).

27. Vendler, review of *Fall*, 203.
28. Pritchard, 593.
29. Quoted in Christensen, "Allen Ginsberg," 239.
30. Shapiro, *Primer for Poets*, 26.
31. Portugés, *Visionary Poetics*, 135.
32. Moore, letter to Ginsberg, 4 July 1952, in *Poetry of Ginsberg*, ed.,
Hyde, 13.
33. *Indian Journals*, 208.

Chapter Eight

1. Interview in Portugés, *Visionary Poetics*, 139.
2. Ibid.
3. Ibid., 135–36.
4. Ibid., 137.
5. Olson, *Human Universe*, 59–60.
6. Portugés, *Visionary Poetics*, 139–61.
7. Beaver, review in *TLS*, 7 July 1978, 754.
8. Hayden Carruth, review of *Mind Breaths*, *New York Times Book Review*, 19 March 1978; reprinted in *Poetry of Ginsberg*, ed. Hyde, 321.
9. Portugés, *Visionary Poetics*, 152–53.
10. Ibid., 154.
11. Ibid., 146–47.
12. Ibid., 141.
13. Ibid., 143.
14. Ibid., 142.
15. William Logan, review of *Plutonian Ode*, *TLS*, 12 November 1982,
125.
16. Paul Berman, review of *Plutonian Ode*, *Village Voice*, 23 March
1982; reprinted in *Poetry of Ginsberg*, ed. Hyde, 362–63.
17. Steven Gould Axelrod, review of *Plutonian Ode*, *World Literature Today* 58 (Winter 1984):104.
18. Kenneth Funsten, review of *Plutonian Ode*, *Los Angeles Times Book Review*, 30 May 1982, 13.

Chapter Nine

1. Beaver, review, 754.
2. Tytell, *Naked Angels,* 4.
3. Ginsberg, Letter to Mark Van Doren, quoted in ibid., 83.
4. Charles Olson, "Under the Mushroom: The Gratwick Highlands Tape," *Olson* 3 (Spring 1975): 43.
5. See Tytell, *Naked Angels,* 213.
6. See Charles Olson, *Poetry and Truth: The Beloit Lectures and Poems,* ed. George Butterick (San Francisco: Four Seasons Foundation, 1971), 6.
7. Olson, *Human Universe,* 4.
8. Ibid., 118.

Selected Bibliography

PRIMARY SOURCES

The following list contains only the major volumes of Ginsberg's poetry, along with a few single items of special significance. Virtually all the poetry published in single volumes has been reprinted in *Collected Poems: 1947–1980*. For a more complete listing of all Ginsberg's published work the reader is directed to Michelle P. Kraus's *Allen Ginsberg: An Annotated Bibliography, 1969–1977*, which supersedes George Dowden's similar compilation. The items are arranged in chronological order of publication.

1. Poetry and Prose

Howl and Other Poems. Pocket Poets Series, no. 4. San Francisco: City Lights Books, 1956.

"Notes Written on Finally Recording *Howl.*" Fantasy Records, Spoken Word Series, 7006, 1959. Reprint. In Thomas Parkinson, *A Casebook On the Beats.* New York: Thomas Y. Crowell, 1961.

"Poetry, Violence and the Trembling Lambs," *Village Voice,* 25 August 1959, 1, 8.

Kaddish and Other Poems 1958–1960. Pocket Poets Series, no. 14. San Francisco: City Lights Books, 1961.

Empty Mirror: Early Poems. New York: Totem Press in Association with Corinth Books, 1961.

The Yage Letters [with William Burroughs]. San Francisco: City Lights Books, 1963.

Reality Sandwiches. Pocket Poets Series, no. 18. San Francisco: City Lights Books, 1963.

Wichita Vortex Sutra. San Francisco: Coyote Books, 1967.

Planet News. San Francisco: City Lights Books, 1968.

T.V. Baby Poems. London: Cape Goliard, 1967. Reprint. New York: Grossman, Orion Press, 1968.

Ankor Wat. London: Fulcrum Press, 1968.

Airplane Dreams: Compositions from Journals. Toronto: Anansi, 1968. Reprint. San Francisco: City Lights Books, 1969.

Notes after an Evening with William Carlos Williams. New York: Samuel Charters, 1970.

Indian Journals: March 1962–May 1963. San Francisco: Dave Haselwood and City Lights Books, 1970.

Ginsberg's Improvised Poetics. Edited by Mark Robison. Buffalo: Anonym Press, 1971.

The Fall of America: Poems of These States 1965–1971. San Francisco: City Lights Books, 1972.

The Gates of Wrath: Rhymed Poems, 1948–1952. Bolinas, Calif.: Grey Fox Press, 1972.

Iron Horse. Toronto: Coach House, 1972. Reprint. San Francisco: City Lights Books, 1974.

Allen Verbatim: Lectures on Poetry, Politics, Consciousness. Edited by Gordon Ball. New York: McGraw-Hill, 1974.

The Visions of the Great Rememberer. Amherst, Mass.: Mulch Press, 1974.

Chicago Trial Testimony. San Francisco: City Lights Books, 1975.

First Blues, Rags, Ballads & Harmonium Songs 1971–74. New Full Court Press, 1975.

To Eberhardt from Ginsberg. Lincoln, Mass.: Penman Press, 1976.

As Ever: The Collected Correspondence of Allen Ginsberg and Neal Cassady. Edited by Barry Gifford. Berkeley, Calif.: Creative Arts, 1977.

Journals: Early Fifties-Early Sixties. Edited by Gordon Ball. New York: Grove Press, 1977.

Poems All Over the Place: Mostly Seventies. Cherry Valley, N.Y.: Cherry Valley Editions, 1978.

Mind Breaths: Poems 1972–1977. San Francisco: City Lights Books, 1978.

Composed on the Tongue. Edited by Donald Allen. Bolinas, Calif.: Grey Fox Press, 1980.

Plutonian Ode. San Francisco: City Lights Books, 1982.

Collected Poems: 1947–1980. New York: Harper & Row, 1984.

White Shroud: Poems 1980–1985. New York: Harper & Row, 1986.

Howl: Original Draft Facsimile. Transcript and Variant Versions. Fully Annotated by Author, with Correspondence, First Readings, Legal Skirmishes, Precursive Text and Bibliography. New York: Harper & Row, 1986.

2. Interviews

Carroll, Paul. *"Playboy* Interview." *Playboy,* April 1969.

Clark, Thomas, "The Art of Poetry VIII," *Paris Review* 37 (Spring 1966). Reprint. In *Writers At Work: The Paris Review Interviews, Third Series,* New York: Viking Press, 1967.

Colbert, Alison. "A Talk with Allen Ginsberg." *Partisan Review* 3 (1971).

Geneson, Paul. "A Conversation with Allen Ginsberg." *Chicago Review* 27 (Summer 1975).

Packard, Williams. "Craft Interview with Allen Ginsberg." In *The Craft of Poetry.* New York: Doubleday, 1974.

Tytell, John. "Conversation with Allen Ginsberg." *Partisan Review* 2 (1974).

Young, Allen. *Gay Sunshine Interview.* Bolinas, Calif.: Grey Fox Press, 1974.

SECONDARY SOURCES

1. Bibliography

Kraus, Michelle P. *Allen Ginsberg: An Annotated Bibliography, 1969–1977.* Metuchen, N.J.: Scarecrow Press, 1980. Supersedes George Dowden's *Bibliography of Works by Allen Ginsberg, October 1943 to July 1967.* Provides a comprehensive catalog of Ginsberg's works and includes the poet's introductory "Contemplation on Bibliography." An invaluable scholarly tool.

2. Books

Charters, Ann. *Scenes along the Road.* New York: Gotham Book Mart, 1970. A photographic study of Ginsberg and other beat writers containing three poems and a commentary by Ginsberg.

Ehrlich, J. W., ed. *Howl of the Censor.* San Carlos, Calif.: Nourse Publishing Co., 1961.

Hyde, Lewis, ed. *On the Poetry of Allen Ginsberg.* Ann Arbor: University of Michigan Press, 1984. An excellent anthology of virtually all important critical reviews and essays on Ginsberg up to 1982. Extremely helpful.

Kramer, Jane. *Allen Ginsberg in America.* New York: Random House, 1968. Expansion of *New Yorker* profile on Ginsberg.

Molesworth, Charles. *The Fierce Embrace: A Study of Contemporary American Poetry.* Columbia: University of Missouri Press, 1979. Sympathetic discussion of Ginsberg as one of the best poets of his generation.

Mottram, Eric. *Allen Ginsberg in the Sixties.* Brighton, England: Unicorn Bookshop, 1972.

Portugés, Paul. *The Visionary Poetics of Allen Ginsberg.* Santa Barbara, Calif.: Ross-Erikson, 1978. A study of Ginsberg's visionary experiences. Contains excellent interviews with Ginsberg.

Rosenthal, M. L. *The New Poets.* New York: Macmillan, 1967. A sound discussion of Ginsberg as a confessional poet.

Tytell, John. *Naked Angels: The Lives & Literature of the Beat Generation.* New York: McGraw-Hill, 1976. Close biographical treatments of Burroughs, Kerouac, and Ginsberg with photographs. Two long sections address Ginsberg. An important, well-researched study.

Index